D0070617

Stories from a Moron

Real Stories
Rejected by
Real Magazines

Ed Broth

St. Martin's Press ✻ New York

NOTE FROM ED BROTH:

I took a few liberties with some of the letters I received from real magazines, deleting some names and addresses and even a line or two, and some are edited. Not a word is added. Real people from real magazines really wrote every word.

www.stmartins.com

Library of Congress Cataloging-in-Publication Data
Broth, Ed.
Stories from a moron : real stories rejected by real magazines / Ed Broth.
p. cm.
ISBN 0-312-32676-9
EAN 978-0312-32676-0

1. American wit and humor. I. Title

PN6165.B76 2004
818'.602—dc22
2004051020

First Edition: January 2005

10 9 8 7 6 5 4 3 2 1

FOREWORD

by Jerry Seinfeld

When I first met Ed Broth we were just killing some time
in a wisecrack bar on a slow section of Melrose Avenue.
It was across the street from a foreign car garage with a
sign that always seemed suspicious, "We fix any foreign
car." If they really could, why would they stop there?

When Broth squared up on you it was Lucite clear
that there was something behind those pool ball eyes and
it wasn't a brain. Oh sure, there was the usual red, gooey
stuff and some veiny things. I'm no ophthalmologist, but
I know one when I see one about once every two years.
When a man rolls up to you on a three-legged luncheon-
ette stool and snugs his little bag of nuts that time forgot
up against your kneecap, you won't need a case of glau-
coma to get a little hazy on the details.

It was 1981 and I eyeballed Broth's waistline at about
thirty-six. In those days they were throwing out the
donut holes instead of sprinkling sugar on them and
shipping them down our gullets. Broth spoke with an
easy Sansabelt style that masked his sharp Haggar
crease wit. He wore glasses and he needed them.
"They're prescription," he used to say to no one in particular as he sipped his rum and coke. And even though
there was never a response no one doubted that they
were. It was classic Broth.

Over the years we remained friends, each of us growing an appropriate amount of weight. I last saw Ed about
a month ago at an industry pastrami joint on a quiet section of Ventura Boulevard. He's up about seventy-five
pounds and that's not a lot. A cruller crumb fell from his

eyelash as he said to me, "You'd be surprised how easy it is to gain seventy-five pounds." And he was right. I was surprised and it did look easy. He told me he was dating a woman that looked like Marv Levy. I said, "The ex-coach of the Buffalo Bills?" He said, "Not Marv Levy, I said Barbara Eden. Can't you hear?" I said, "No, I just came from the ophthalmologist. Whatever she looks like, it's better than losing four Super Bowls." And he had to admit maybe this time I was right.

We agreed to get together on a regular basis and even though we didn't it was nice to agree on something. "What for?" I said. "The only thing we've come up with after twenty years of gibberish talk is Strawberry People." (Strawberry People is Broth's idea for a possible third alternative to heterosexuality or homosexuality, the only current options.) Strawberry People wouldn't work and doesn't make sense, but anyone that hears it is forced to admit that at least someone has attempted to come up with something, some kind of third flavor that could be at least discussed as a solution to our relationship problems.

And I think that's the best way I can describe Broth's stories. They don't completely make sense, but they don't make nonsense either. It's a third flavor. It's not a meal and it's not a drink, it's Broth. It can warm your insides or stain your tie. So whether you eat it up with a spoon or go face down and asphyxiate yourself, by the time you're done you'll feel like you've got a shine on your shoes, nuts on your knee and a song in your heart.

Welcome to the world of Ed Broth. I think we could all use a warm, clear liquid with a faintly chickenish smell right about now.

DEDICATION AND ACKNOWLEDGMENTS

Dedicated to Rita Marder

Top of the Line Thanks to: Elizabeth Beier, Dan Strone, Phyllis Murphy. A sensational group of people that rate a Top of the Line Thanks which I normally do not give out. (Except sparingly.)

Exalted Thanks to: Morris Marder, Justin Siegel, Sharon Siegel, Linda Shaw (my dear), Johnny Dark, Hilary Rubin, Michael Connor, Jessica Seinfeld, Kevin Dochtermann, Dr. Melvin Weisberg, Jeanne Schwartz, Cookie Saltzburg, Bert Saltzburg, Dr. Mark Gerard, Dr. Theodore Goldstein, Dr. Douglas Shreck, Dr. Michael Robbins, Dr. Libed, Heather Florence, Erin McPherson, Neil Meyer, Sam Dansky, Marilyn Deutsch, Cele Braverman, Whitey and Annette Marder, Nancy Marder, Sun Ray, Poopsie, Stanley Abrams, Hershel Pearl, Kenneth Braun, Peanut the dachshund (fine dog, really), Karen and Bret Bachman, Gail Kringold, Larry Hankoff, Jeff Mahl, Jack Weiner, Sally Ruskin, Vivian Greene, Gladys Young, Andy Jonas, Karen Myers, Robyn Marks, Abby, Rick, David, Chas, and Marge Chereton, Richard Daar, Bill, Helen, Resa, and Alyson Brody, Leslie Pine, Mrs. Harriet Glick, Dr. Elizabeth Reeves, Dr. Myron Tong, Melody Marder, Dr Curt Oleson, Amery Wirtshafter, Beth Levy, Leonore and Florence Grudner, Bill Wollman, and Jerry's Deli, Robbin Stubbs, Abbi, Billy, Al, Ritchie, Jennifer, Barbi, Jen, Monica, Bridgette, Michele, Tara, Shauna.

And . . . a Four-Star, Gold Circle, Platinum Club, Colonel's Staff, Admiral's Nest, Captain's Crunch, Award-Winning Members Only Special Diamond Plateau Thanks to: Jerry Seinfeld.

Stories of
Hope
and
Inspiration

HOTEL HONOR BAR

I am a traveling salesman. A pretty good one. I think. I work my route going from town to town setting up franchises. I drive a Buick Ravioli. This is Buick's sporty little go anywhere car. I like it very much. Sometimes I bring a heavy woman with me for company. Her name is Cheryl Glimpsey and she goes with me on the road. Cheryl helped me fix a flat tire recently on my car. Well, let me tell you what happened. We were driving and my tire blew out. Luckily she had a product called "PATCH A FLAT". This is a goo that you spray from a can into your flat tire and it inflates the tire. Well, while fixing that flat, the tire blew up in her face and her eyeball flew out. Luckily she also had a can of "PATCH AN EYE." That's what life on the road is like for a traveling salesman like myself. I am Ed Broth.

I work for the "SOCK 'N SHOE RESTAURANTS". This is a theme restaurant where your meal is brought to the table in a shoe and your bread is wrapped in a sock. They are very popular in Tuscasquelga, Mississippi where there are 47 of them in a 5 block radius. Chain restaurants have exploded in the new millennium and this millennium was no exception. The full name of this very fine chain is "FRED MAROON'S ORIGINAL SOCK 'N SHOE RESTAURANT". Fred made his fortune from a shoe store and he figured the natural transition would be to open a restaurant with the leftover stock. At our last corporate function Fred sat there with unwashed slacks and a back full of rooster bites and said he got them from an unclean theme park pirate ride. I didn't believe him. I always thought it was from all that damn taffy he ate. Fred once stood up in a motel lobby and yelled out MY SANDWICH HAS NO TASTE!! He stood there for 45 min-

utes in the lobby and just yelled out MY SANDWICH HAS
NO TASTE!! He just yelled that over and over again.
Finally it got very quiet. Like in the movie The Hound of
the Baskervilles. It was an eerie stillness. Then finally
someone else from across the lobby yelled out: THEN GET
A NEW SANDWICH!!!

On this sales trip I checked into the HYAT QUAN DUC
THUONG HOTEL in Tweetie, Arizona. I must say here
that the Hyat Hotel Chain is the finest out there. They
cater to your every need. This is a 4 star, Triple A-,
Chevco Award Winner, prestigious, luxury hotel with
shuttle service every 35 seconds to a ditch. I once rode
their courtesy bus for an hour before I had to get off and
use the Dairy Knave restroom. It was so filthy I saw a
cockroach with a mop in its hand.

Upon checking into my room at the Hyat Quan Duc
Thoung Hotel I immediately noticed they had an HONOR
BAR in the hotel room. Some hotels call it a MINI BAR.
This is a little bar filled with candy and soda, and pretzels, and drinks all for sale. It is locked and comes with a
key. I am at a continuing loss as to why they still have to
lock up soda and candy for an adult. Is there that much
abuse here?

I must say that the Honor Bar prices are very steep.
$7.00 for a soda, $5.00 for a candy bar, $10.00 for a jar
of Spanish nuts. I am a reasonable traveler, expecting to
pay for the service of having a fully loaded assortment of
goodies in my room at the ready after a night of partying
with heavy people but these prices are way high.

To continue my story: I added up everything in the
Honor Bar and realized I had $3,000.00 worth of candy
and soda in my room. I did not feel comfortable with this
many valuables in the room. So I called the front desk
and asked if they could put my candy and soda in the
hotel safe. They said they would accommodate me. "It's

the smart thing to do, Mr. Broth," they said, as I hung up the phone and burned my comforter. (For sanitary reasons). I once saw a cockroach commit suicide on a hotel comforter because of the filth. He hung himself with some dental floss.

The front desk sent a Security Guard up to my room and we emptied the Honor Bar contents into a Wells Fargo security bag. (Large bag of Funions, Ludens cough drops, Mesquite fudgeslops, Nutrageous candy bar, crabapple Snapple, small Captain Morgans Bay Rum). We then left the room together, he with a loaded gun at his hip, and he walked me and my candy down to the lobby and to the hotel safe where I deposited my mini bar items.

He gave me a professional nod and I gave him a courtesy half smile as I exited the lobby. I looked back and I noticed that he was adjusting his trousers. They must have scrunched up on him during our walk. I make it a habit of noticing many security guards trousers scrunch up on them as they walk. Take a look yourself and see if it's not true.

I felt better. All I had in my room now was my platinum watch, diamond ring, a few thousand dollars, and a cell phone with 19,000 unused minutes on it. Far less valuable then the soda and Spanish nuts that were now secured safely in the hotel safe.

I will continue this story later.

CONJUGAL CAL

When I was a youngster my cousin Phillipe told me his Uncle Bosco used to read to him a book called "CONJUGAL CAL FROM CALICO COVE". It was about the adventures of Conjugal Cal, a prisoner with a big red moustache and thinning red hair who used to have conjugal visits while he was incarcerated. He had a girlfriend named Marga-reetio. Conjugal Cal was from Calico Cove which was a small town where Cal got into trouble stealing things and was sent to prison. Phillipe said he loved the little stories and they helped him fall asleep.

Years later when I was asked to write my own short stories I remembered Conjugal Cal and his many adventures in that tiny trailer on the prison grounds that Phillipe used to tell me about. I tried to contact Phillipe but I was told he had fled the United States and I was not to try and find him. His Uncle Bosco had moved on to a respectable position as a water delivery man and did not want to discuss his cousin anymore but yes, Uncle Bosco did remember the Conjugal Cal stories and he did not mind if I used them. Let me read to you one of Conjugal Cal's adventures:

USED WITH PERMISSION FROM "CONJUGAL CAL FROM CALICO COVE."

FROM THE BOOK: It was a hot humid day at Bushy Mountain Prison in North Carolina. The sky was bright because the sun was shining. When the sun was shining the sky was usually bright. The prisoners were milling around in the exercise yard. Some were lifting weights, some were playing dominoes with buttons, one was staggering across the yard clutching his arm, two were posing. (One had a funny little hat on.) All the prisoners were busy on the yard. All except one. Conjugal Cal. He was in his little trailer on the prison grounds waiting for a visit from his sweetie, Margareetio. It was 8 in the morning and although a little early, it was the time that the Warden scheduled for Cal.

"I have many prisoners here besides you, Cal, that need to be serviced. They need sex like you too or else they will explode if they don't blow off a little steam. Some hold their arm. I'm sorry. Next time I'll schedule you for a nooner," the Warden said to Conjugal Cal.

"That's OK, Warden, you won't hear a peep out of me. Except for later around 10:15 when I make a grunt and a bleep."

Now many prisoners wait for that conjugal visit. That time when they can be reunited with their girlfriend or wife and enjoy themselves as before when they were free men. Not the sickness that goes on in prison today that you see on a cable show 75 times a week. Not that sickness which I can only watch 50 minutes of before I have to turn it off in disgust. (And believe me I have been disgusted many times. As many as 75 times in a week.)

Margareetio arrived at 7:3Q in the morning on the bus. She had on a sparkly dress. Some of the sparkles shook off as she moved down the bus steps. She was a big woman and the dress had many sparkles. When a big woman moves sparklies fly off. She was driven to the prison in a Comfort Inn Courtesy Van. She opened the door to that tiny trailer that was near the Warden's home with his prison curtains in the window and Conjugal Cal had a big smile on his face. "Margareetio, give me a fat sloppy kiss," he said. "Get on over here, big woman. Save some sparkles for me." (Some more sparklies fell off as she went over to Conjugal Cal.)

The Warden kept an eye on his prisoner as they both went into that tiny trailer. Who knows what went on in there? Huh?

NOTE TO READER: Now was the time when I was a lad that Phillipe told me he drifted off to sleep and Uncle Bosco would say "You missed a lot of the story." And sleepy Phillipe would say, "What happened?" Phillipe said he was tired for many years and never really got much past this part that I just read to you. Once he said he made it to a few pages more to a viscous argument between Margareetio and Conjugal Cal where she said "I won't do that" and "That's disgusting" and "Phooey." But that was it. His Uncle Bosco never read further to little Phillipe from that book.

The Conjugal Cal books were published in 64 languages and became best sellers in Germany. Eventually they were made into a movie there with Tom Cruise turning down the part of Conjugal Cal. In my letters to Tom Cruise (there were 12 of them) I suggested that he made a bad career move by not playing Conjugal Cal. After all they were both frisky people. And the books were big sellers. To date he has not answered me.

NEW CLOTHESLINE

I just bought a new clothesline a month ago. The receipt said September 5, 2002. It is a very nice clothesline, sturdy like a clothesline should be. I am very happy with it. And every morning I hang my shorty pajamas up to dry after I wash them out in my sink. My clothesline is a few feet from my new neighbor's house.

After about a month of this my new neighbor came to me and said that he and his family are finding it nauseating that they eat their dinner every night and have to look at my shorty pajamas. They said that night after night they sit as a family and talk about their life—their successes, their hopes, their dreams, their goals, and they look up and see my shorty pajamas flapping away at them, almost like my pajamas were waving to them.

I said "Well, I am sorry but my pajamas get very stinky at night and I wash them out in my sink and that they have to dry somewhere. Don't they?" I went on to tell him that in no way are my pajamas waving to him. "That would be impossible, wouldn't it?" I said. "Especially shorties. Shorties don't wave to people, do they?" What is he insane?

The next night I had my shorty pajamas flapping on the line as usual—they are stinky and get dirty and need to be washed and dried that is why I bought a clothesline—when I noticed my neighbor and his family eating dinner. I think I could make out some sort of stew. There were potatoes and carrots and peas in his food. To me that is a stew. Something I have argued about with my new neighbor in the past.

My neighbor rushed out to me as I was putting my shorty pajamas on my new clothesline. My neighbor was pasty faced and his hair was matted. I think his name is

Frank. Frank Tint. He must be European, maybe Scandinavian or something as I have never heard that name before. Something I have mentioned to him in the past.

He said to me that he was convinced that my shorty pajamas flapping and waving to him were the Devil and that they were taking over his and his family's life. He said his hopes and dreams and aspirations as a family were destroyed by my shorty pajamas.

I said "Nonsense. How could my shorty pajamas be the Devil? They are simply shorty pajamas that I got dirty from sleeping in. I am just washing out my evening sleep wear—that's all!" I told him. "Furthermore, I said, "They Were NOT the Devil and they are not talking to him." These are simply stinky shorty pajamas that I sleep in every night and that I wash out every morning so I can sleep in them at night. That's all. I went back into my house to make myself a sandwich. (Low carb salami)

A few days later, I noticed my neighbor and his family eating again. I think they were having lots of eggs. I couldn't be sure. But it appeared to be he had 37 hard-boiled eggs on his plate in front of him. (Again, we argued about this.) He was furiously peppering them. My shorty pajamas were on the clothesline, flapping in the wind at his family. It was pretty windy and they were really flapping. They were getting dry. This was probably the most flapping I had seen them do. The sky was starting to get dark. It was getting overcast. I had seen this same sky before in a Lou Diamond Phillips alien abduction movie. I could tell that my neighbor's whole family was being overtaken by a strange force as I looked through the window. My dirty pajamas waved to them as his family danced in the window. He waved back at me with his egg stained fork. He had pepper on his face. I do not like these neighbors. Phooey!

There was definitely something creepy going on with that family and they were trying to blame it on my dirty, stinky shorty pajamas. Who were they do do that? Who are they to cast aspersions at me? Huh? I am just a new neighbor with a new clothesline doing my wash; cleaning my pajamas. They get stinky.

I took my NOW CLEAN shorty pajamas into my house and closed my curtains. I made a note to throw a rock at his car. His name is Frank Tint. (As I have mentioned.)

ENDO

Fencing Gear For the Brain

FENCERS QUARTERLY MAGAZINE

848 S. Kimbrough,
Springfield, MO 65806

January 8, 2003

Hello Ed,

Sorry. This submission is not right for *Fencers Quarterly*. As our name implies, we focus on and publish material related to the sport of fencing. We are definitely *not* a general interest magazine. As far as I can tell, your story has nothing to with fencing.

As a word of advice, it always helps for writers to be familiar with the publications they submit material to. I am enclosing a copy of one of our past issues to give you an idea of what we do publish.

Sincerely,

Nick Evangelista

Nick Evangelista

Editor-in-Chief, *FQM*

ED BROTH
10153 ½ Riverside Dr.
#241
Toluca Lake, CA 91602

Mr. Nick Evangelista
Editor, Fencers Quarterly Magazine
848 S. Kimbrough
Springfield, MO 65806

1/14/03

Dear Editor Evangelista,

Thank you for taking the time to point out some writing advice to me; namely that my story "NEW CLOTHESLINE" had nothing to do with fencing. I read your magazine cover to cover especially your EDITORS COLUMN and enjoyed the photos in your magazine. I have fixed my story to include the fencing angle it always should have had. I hope you like!

With Respect,

Ed Broth

Ed Broth
Fencer

NEW CLOTHESLINE

I just bought a new clothesline a month ago. The receipt said September 5, 2002. It is a very nice clothesline, sturdy like a clothesline should be. I am very happy with it. And every morning I hang my shorty pajamas up to dry after I wash them out in my sink. My clothesline is a few feet from my new neighbor's house.

After about a month of this my new neighbor came to me and said that he and his family are finding it nause-ating that they eat their dinner every night and have to look at my shorty pajamas. They said that night after night they sit as a family and talk about their life—their successes, their hopes, their dreams, their goals, and they look up and see my shorty pajamas flapping away at them, almost like my pajamas were waving to them.

I said "Well, I am sorry but my pajamas get very stinky at night and I wash them out in my sink and that they have to dry somewhere. Don't they?" I went on to tell him that in no way are my pajamas waving to him.

"That would be impossible, wouldn't it?" I said. "Especially shorties. Shorties don't wave to people, do they?" What is he insane?

The next night I had my shorty pajamas flapping on the line as usual—they are stinky and get dirty and need to be washed and dried that is why I bought a clothesline—when I noticed my neighbor and his family eating dinner. I think I could make out some sort of stew. There were potatoes and carrots and peas in his food. To me that is a stew. Something I have argued about with my new neighbor in the past.

My neighbor rushed out to me as I was putting my shorty pajamas on my new clothesline. My neighbor was pasty faced and his hair was matted. I think his name is Frank. Frank Tint. He must be European, maybe Scandinavian or something as I have never heard that name before. Something I have mentioned to him in the past.

He said to me that he was convinced that my shorty pajamas flapping and waving to him were the Devil and that they were taking over his and his family's life. He said his hopes and dreams and aspirations as a family were destroyed by my shorty pajamas.

I said "Nonsense. How could my shorty pajamas be the Devil? They are simply shorty pajamas that I got dirty from sleeping in. I am just washing out my evening

sleep wear—that's all!" I told him. "Furthermore, I said, "They Were NOT the Devil and they are not talking to him." These are simply stinky shorty pajamas that I sleep in every night and that I wash out every morning so I can sleep in them at night. That's all. I went back into my house to make myself a sandwich. (Low carb salami)

A few days later, I noticed my neighbor and his family eating again. I think they were having lots of eggs. I couldn't be sure. But it appeared to be he had 37 hard-boiled eggs on his plate in front of him. (Again, we argued about this.) He was furiously peppering them. My shorty pajamas were on the clothesline, flapping in the wind at his family. It was pretty windy and they were really flapping. They were getting dry. This was probably the most flapping I had seen them do. The sky was starting to get dark. It was getting overcast. I had seen this same sky before in a Lou Diamond Phillips alien abduction movie. I could tell that my neighbor's whole family was being overtaken by a strange force as I looked through the window. My dirty pajamas waved to them as his family danced in the window. He waved back at me with his egg stained fork. He had pepper on his face. I do not like these neighbors. Fooey!

There was definitely something creepy going on with that family and they were trying to blame it on my dirty, stinky shorty pajamas. Who were they do do that? Who are they to cast aspersions at me? Huh? I am just a new neighbor with a new clothesline doing my wash; cleaning my pajamas. They get stinky.

I took my NOW CLEAN shorty pajamas into my house and closed my curtains. I made a note to throw a rock at his car. His name is Frank Tint. (As I have mentioned.)

ENDO

Fencers Quarterly Magazine

848 S KIMBROUGH
SPRINGFIELD, MO 65806
EDITOR@FENCERSQUARTERLY.COM

Dear Ed:

I'm not sure whether to laugh or cry.

First off, this piece is utterly, utterly wrong for FQM. We don't do fiction/humor/memoirs unless they are related to FENCING. Snagging a couple photocopies ▓▓▓▓▓▓▓▓ from FQM's pages (which is copyright infringement, a serious crime, I might note), and pasting them into a piece that has nothing to do with fencing, does not make it fencing-related. *This is the same non-fencing piece you sent before!*

Second, I'm going to cut you some slack -- but not much. You've clearly gotten the basics of article submittal: you did a cover letter and sent an SASE. The story itself is offbeat and funny, showing that you've got some writing ability. But I can assure you that you are not targeting the correct market for your work. After "reading from cover to cover" you should be perfectly clear that your piece is not going to fly at FQM -- there is nothing even remotely like it in any previous issue (and there won't be anything like it in any subsequent issue, either)! Basically, you just wasted your money and my time.

Third, I'm encouraging you to send your material to an appropriate market -- if you don't already have a copy, you should purchase a *Writer's Market* (amazon.com, barnesandnoble.com and your local bookstore all have copies), or check it out at your local library. Look for humor markets, and send your article there. And remember to double-space it!

Finally, I will look at future material, BUT if it's not fencing-related, I'll send it back without any comment. 'Nuff said?

Perturbed,

Nick Evangelista

Nick Evangelista
Editor-in-Chief
FENCERS QUARTERLY

ED BROTH
10153½ Riverside Dr.
#241
Toluca Lake, CA 91602

Mr. Nick Evangelista
Editor, Fencers Quarterly Magazine
848 S. Kimbrough
Springfield, M. 65806

1/24/03

Dear Editor Evangelista,

Please let me start off by sincerely thanking you for taking the
time to guide me correctly. Please don't let me perturb you. I
sincerely appreciate that you take the time to help me with my
story. And that you like my work. I am encouraged.
     Now: Forget the clothesline story. Just forget it. After
rereading it, it is not right for Fencing Quarterly Magazine. (I am
convinced of that—you pointed it out to me) I sent it on to
STEAMBOAT MAGAZINE. Perhaps they will like it.
     Encouraged by you, I am enclosing a completely new story
which I believe captures fencing and would be suitable for your
readers. It is called "CONJUGAL CAL" and it really is about
fencing. Fencing is really a lot in this story. (There's lots of fencing
in here is what I'm saying). I highlighted in bold and underlined
the fencing in the story.
     I was also thinking . . . I would like to inquire about placing an
ad in your magazine for my business. Because I like your
magazine, I think an ad would be good for my business. Please tell
me the cost of this. I hope you like my new story. You're a nice
man.

With Utter Respect,

Ed Broth

Ed Broth

January 17, 2003

Ed Broth
10153 1/2 Riverside Drive
#241
Toluca Lake, CA 91602

Dear Ed:

   Thank you for your recent submission to *Steamboat Magazine*, it was wonderful to hear how much our magazine has touched you. As you may know, our publication is printed semiannually and so accepts relatively few freelance articles per year. Unfortunately at present, we do not have a space that would be appropriate for your work.
   I am enclosing a copy of our writers' guidelines for your use with future queries. We hope to hear from you again, should you have a story idea that you think might work for us.

Thank you,

Editor

STEAMBOAT MAGAZINE

CONJUGAL CAL

When I was a youngster my cousin Phillipe told me his Uncle Bosco used to read to him a book called "CONJUGAL CAL FROM CALICO COVE". It was about the adventures of Conjugal Cal, a prisoner with a big red moustache and thinning red hair who used to have conjugal visits while he was incarcerated. He had a girlfriend named Margareetio. Conjugal Cal was from Calico Cove which was a small town where Cal got into trouble stealing things and was sent to prison. Phillipe said he loved the little stories and they helped him fall asleep.

Years later when I was asked to write my own short stories I remembered Conjugal Cal and his many adventures in that tiny trailer on the prison grounds that Phillipe used to tell me about. I tried to contact Phillipe but I was told he had fled the United States and I was not to try and find him. His Uncle Bosco had moved on to a respectable position as a water delivery man and did not want to discuss his cousin anymore but yes, Uncle Bosco did remember the Conjugal Cal stories and he did not mind if I used them. Let me read to you one of Conjugal Cal's adventures:

USED WITH PERMISSION FROM "CONJUGAL CAL FROM CALIFO COVE."

FROM THE BOOK: It was a hot humid day at Bushy Mountain Prison in North Carolina. The sky was bright because the sun was shining. When the sun was shining the sky was usually bright. The prisoners were milling around in the exercise yard. Some were lifting weights, some were playing dominoes with buttons, one was staggering across the yard clutching his arm, two were pos-

ing. (One had a funny little hat on.) **One had fencing gear on.** All the prisoners were busy on the
yard. All except one. Conjugal Cal. He was in his
little trailer on the prison grounds waiting for a
visit from his sweetie, Margareetio. It was 8 in the
morning and although a little early, it was the
time that the Warden scheduled for Cal.

"I have many prisoners here besides you, Cal,
that need to be serviced. They need sex like you
too or else they will explode if they don't blow off
a little steam. Some hold their arm. I'm sorry.
Next time I'll schedule you for a nooner," the Warden said to Conjugal Cal.

"That's OK, Warden, you won't hear a peep out
of me. Except for later around 10:15 when I make
a grunt and a bleep."

**Now the Warden was busy with his fencing
team. He had lined them all up to engage in a
prison fencing match. There must have been 71
prisoners out there by the conjugal visit trailer all
of them ready to go at it against each other with
their sharp swords and mesh masks. One prisoner's name was Maestro Funches Jr. who many
believed was related to the Grand Master Fencing
Champeen. Oh, the fencers were having a grand
time ready to engage in a grand sport on this grand
sunny day.**

Now many prisoners wait for that conjugal
visit. That time when they can be reunited with
their girlfriend or wife and enjoy themselves as
before when they were free men. Not the sickness
that goes on in prison today that you see on a
cable show 75 times a week. Not that sickness
which I can only watch 50 minutes of before I
have to turn it off in disgust. (And believe me I

have been disgusted many times. As many as 75 times in a week.)

Margareetio arrived at 7:30 in the morning on the bus. She had on a sparkly dress. Some of the sparkles shook off as she moved down the bus steps. She was a big woman and the dress had many sparkles. When a big woman moves sparklies fly off. She was driven to the prison in a Comfort Inn Courtesy Van. She opened the door to that tiny trailer that was near the Warden's **clothesline with his prison skiivies flapping on them** and Conjugal Cal had a big smile on his face. "Margareetio, give me a fat sloppy kiss," he said. "Get on over here, big woman. Save some sparkles for me." (Some more sparklies fell off as she went over to Conjugal Cal.)

The Warden kept an eye on his prisoner as they both went into that tiny trailer. Who knows what went on in there? Huh? **But the Warden also kept an eye on his fencing team which was assembled by the clothesline where the Warden's undies were hanging and flapping. They were really flapping. The sky was starting to get dark. The prison fencers were really going at it fencing away. Swish! Swoosh! Swash! went their swords as they parried and swiveled about getting dangerously close to the Warden's clothesline with his underwear on it flapping away. Almost like they were waving.**

Conjugal Cal yelled out from his trailer: "Hey, you wanna knock off that fencing noise out there. We're trying to have sex in here!!!

NOTE TO READER: Now was the time when I was a lad that Phillipe told me he drifted off to sleep and Uncle Bosco would say "You missed a lot of the story." And sleepy Phillipe would say, "What happened?" Phillipe said he was tired for many years and never really got much past this part that I just read to you. Once he said he made it to a few pages more to a viscous argument between Margareetio and Conjugal Cal where she said "I won't do that" and "That's disgusting" and "Phooey." But that was it. His Uncle Bosco never read further to little Phillipe from that book.

The Conjugal Cal books were published in 64 languages and became best sellers in Germany. Eventually they were made into a movie there with Tom Cruise turning down the part of Conjugal Cal. In my letters to Tom Cruise (there were 12 of them) I suggested that he made a bad career move by not playing Conjugal Cal. After all they were both frisky people. And the books were big sellers. To date he has not answered me.

Fencing Gear For the Brain

FENCERS QUARTERLY
MAGAZINE

848 S. Kimbrough,
Springfield, MO 65806

February 5, 2003

Ed Broth
10153 1/2 Riverside Dr, #241
Toluca Lake, CA 91602

Dear Ed:

Your piece is not appropriate for our magazine. We do not publish stories about individuals like Conjugal Cal, or about underwear -- no matter how often references are made to fencing. *Referring* to fencing is not the same as writing an article or story *about* fencing. Please look very thoroughly at the issue of FQM which I sent to you. You will notice that there are NO fiction pieces, NO humor pieces, and NO articles which deviate significantly from the topic of fencing. This is a *fencing* magazine.

You indicate in your letter of 1/31/03 that you wish to "place a story." This is an admirable effort, and we wish you success. However, you cannot sell a story where it will not fit. Your stories do not fit our magazine. You cannot *make* a story about convicts or underwear fit our magazine, even if the convicts "fence." It is obvious that the story's allusions to fencing were included in an attempt to place the piece in FQM (i.e., the reference to "Maestro Jr."). Underlining and bolding those portions was wasted effort.

Your expressed interest in advertising in FQM appears spurious, as well. As you will note by looking at the ads in the issue we sent you, all the advertisers offer items specific to fencing. In good conscience, we cannot accept advertising that is not related to fencing -- and, since you are not a fencer and don't have a business related to fencing, there's not much point in placing an ad in FQM. Subscription forms are in the magazine, if you really wish to subscribe.

I will not address your comments about whether the previous story was "entirely new" or not, nor your remarks about the turnaround time on our mail, nor on which day we typed our replies. However, I will address the fact that *arguing with an editor about trivialities* does not endear you to him.

Seriously, Ed -- you are articulate, use grammar correctly, follow protocol when you make a submission, and apparently can write. How can you be so utterly mistaken about where you send your stories? No amount of wishing, or hoping, or trying to manipulate an editor is going to sell a story where it won't fit. *You must write a story that is appropriate to the market* -- that is the only way you will make sales.

You've had three tries here at FQM. I think that we've given you a fair opportunity to be heard, and we've provided clear and articulate reasons why your work will not be published here. I hope you will take these suggestions to heart, continue writing, and focus your work so that you can begin to see the sales you want. Please realize that I won't be giving you any further advice.

Sincerely,

Nick Evangelista

Nick Evangelista
Editor-in-Chief
FQM

MY BACKGROUND

I was born in Cumberland County. Daddy was insane. Let me just tell you that. His daddy before him was insane. And his daddy's daddy was insane. Their daddy's were all insane. Every man in my family was insane. They just weren't right. This had gone back in my family to the year 1612. We were riddled with insanity. Then it was a normal Daddy, 2 chubby men, a big guy named Roy, then a midsize man about 160 pounds, then in 1217 another insane guy, then there were three more insanes, another normal guy (we think—could have been insane), a giant, and then an insane again. (I think his name was Perry).

I am not insane. I am normal.

I must have got the genes from the chubby guy in 1612. But I loved my Daddy even though he was insane. I grew to be a sturdy man with a corn cob pipe and a felt hat. I am an example of a fully developed man. Some of us are just lucky. Daddy's name was Brad. Someone once told me he was named after the metal fastener that holds pages together in a report. Daddy never mentioned this to me. He just said he name was Brad and that was that. We accepted it. He was the best Daddy. He wore his shirt out a lot. He had mustard on his face.

Daddy worked in Cumberland County at the "THE MOIST MULE RESTAURANT". It was a family owned and family run and family customer restaurant specializing in family fare. They specialized in Mule Melts. ("We Leave the Hair Between the Ears On"—that was their slogan on the menu.) It was originally called "THE MOIST BURRO" but no one showed up and it almost went out of business until they changed the name to mule then everyone came like crazy. It was overnight. On Monday it was "THE MOIST BURRO" and the place was empty. The next night, Tuesday, with the name change to MOIST MULE there were 500 people in the restaurant. And another 200 lined up around the block! The "MOIST MULE" was Cumberland County's premier dining establishment. They catered to the elite from weddings to corporate functions to graduations. We once had an Iranian dignitary eat here and he belched up a fig and used the restroom 15 times. I fluttered my eyes. The manager was Ray. Ray Glimpsey was his full name but everybody just called him Ray. He was no relation to Cheryl Glimpsey the chubby woman who accompanied me on trips around the Sacramento sunbelt. Ray was at the front podium when you first go into the restaurant. Ray was dressed in a diaper and a bonnet. Ray was in his 40's and I remember him from the Pep Guys on Route 7 where he was a service manager who was let go when a car fell on an older lady. He was showing her the undercoating and the car loosened and fell on her. The woman was very elegant, silver hair, slender nose, long gloves, that sort of thing. That car flattened her like a Haitian pancake. Now Ray was working as Manager at the "Moist Mule". Ray was a slight man so the diaper fit kind of loose. Some diapers on 47 year old men fit a little snug but Ray looked kinda just OK in his diaper. Ray once ate 65 bananas but lost the employee contest anyway. He swore he would never eat another banana but the next day he was back eating bananas.

Mamma was a lilliputian. A lilliputian is a small person, not quite a dwarf but still considered to be in the dwarf family. She was the best Mamma a boy could have growing up in Cumberland County. Mama was under 3 feet. Her mamma before her was a lilliputian and her mamma's mamma was a lilliputian. This went back into our family until the year 1205 then it was a normal mother, then 2 more lilliputians, a giant woman, another lilliputian, and then a small man also named Brad. (Again named for the metal fastener used with 3 hole punch paper)

I enjoyed my childhood in Cumberland County and am very proud of my parents. We had a normal childhood in every way. Daddy worked hard and always treated Mamma like a queen bringing her home flowers and gifts every night. Mamma had at one time 35 boxes of unopened candy just when she said she could not eat any more candy. Then she ate more candy. Daddy also brought her a new bracelet almost every year, fine dresses, and a vacuum. The three of us made a fine family, my Daddy the insane, my mother the lilliputian, and me—a sandy haired, freckled faced, strawberry eatin' gimp. I was a well adjusted boy; happy in every way. Daddy used to carry around scallops in a plastic baggy. Everywhere he went he carried around those scallops. I think there were three of them. They were round and whitish and one day I said, "Daddy, your scallops smell. They're stinky. Whatcha doin' with 'em?" He said, "I don't know." And then he threw them away. He never carried them around anymore. Oh sure one time I saw a plastic bag peeping out from under his mattress with what appeared to be a scallop in it, but I couldn't be sure. It was not my nature to peek under Daddy's mattress. I just accepted that my Daddy USED to carry scallops in a baggy. And that was that.*

Cumberland County was a great place to grow up with its clumps of dirt. I took many hayrides. I had a dog named Teenie. Teenie had a white spot on her head. I want to stress here we had a normal healthy happy

---

*Scallops get very stinky under a bed.

childhood, normal in every way with loving parents and a warm environment. I had a pony. We always had shoes, toys, a new refrigerator, plenty of food, gifts of all kind. My dog was special. Teenie was a miniature Chihuahua, weighing about 4 ounces, very tiny, that's why we called her Teenie. She licked me a lot when I was a boy. Daddy worked hard, came home every night, and was there for his family. Mamma was good people. That was my childhood growing up in Cumberland County.

MAILING ADDRESS
Please send all submissions to:

Editor
Young & Alive
PO Box 6097
Lincoln, NE 68506

Young & Alive is published by Christian Record Services, Inc.

Due to a current overabundance of manuscripts, we regret to inform you we will not be accepting any additional manuscripts until the year 2009. Please feel free to resubmit your article at that time for appraisal.

editor

Christian Record Services

DADDY WAS A KLEPTOMANIAC

Daddy stole when I was growing up. Everything we had
he stole. He was a kleptomaniac. We didn't know the term
for it then but we know it now. He was sick. We knew he
was insane but to what point? Stealing? Every day Daddy
stole a box of candy from the local "SEEZES CANDY" that
was in town. He would walk into that Seezes, look around,
yell "Over here!" then when the sales lady would come
over to help Daddy he would show them a squished cream
filled candy on the floor (that he dropped) and while she
was cleaning it up he would swipe a 1 pound box of fancy
chocolates. He would give it to Mamma. This went on 35
times. (In a month) Always with the same dropped Seezes
candy. Sometimes it was a maple filling, sometimes it was
raspberry but he always yelled "Over here! and the same
sales gal would come over and see the squished cream
filled candy on the floor and clean it up while Daddy
walked out of the store with a 1 pounder. I think her
name was Irene. Irene Wobble. They always gave you free
samples at Seezes. Daddy stole those too. And when
Seezes Candy opened "SEEZES OINTMENTS" and they sold
not only cream filled candies but chocolate covered rash
ointment Daddy stole some Seezes ointment too. The
"SEEZES OLD FASHIONED OINTMENT SHOPPE" had the
same older lady on the front of it and the same homey at-
mosphere except they sold boil ointments and heat rash
salve instead of cream filled candies. Seezes had the best
candy in Cumberland County. Years later we were told
that the ointment Seezes and the candy Seezes may have
been run by different people. But who cares?

"Seezes Good Old Fashioned Chafing Ointment". That
was their slogan. Their nougatty ointment and soft center
ointment really cleared up Daddy's boils. When Mamma

asked Daddy where he got his boils from he said, "I don't know," and Mamma said under her breath, "He must have stole them boils."

Daddy stole the following things: Scallops, a Chihuahua named Teenie, a pony, mattress, 35 boxes of candy, swing set, new bracelet, fine dress, vacuum. He was a sick, pathetic man. Daddy once stole a refrigerator from "WILSON APPLIANCE" on Main Street. In Cumberland County. And gave it to Mamma for Christmas. He carried that refrigerator home by himself on his insane body like an ant with a piece of yellow cake. We put that refrigerator next to a freezer daddy stole from a Game Show. One day Daddy came home with a swing set and the next hour a man followed him home with a shotgun and took back that swing set. The man had a bushy red beard, red hair, and big red bushy eyebrows. Later on Daddy helped him with his Singles Ad. He met a creep.

Oh Daddy was sick alright but he provided for us. We got new shoes every year, a new refrigerator on Christmas and a swing set for an hour. Daddy used to say "If life gives you a dilemma, then make De lemonade."

August 19, 1999

Dear. *writer*

Please be advised that we have not published Sugah magazine in over 3 years. The magazines we do publish are: Gent, Nugget, Plumpers & Big Women, Petite and Dude. Thank you for your interest in our magazines.

Sincerely,

ED BROTH
10153 ½ Riverside Dr.
#241
Toluca Lake, CA 91602

Editor, STEAMBOAT MAGAZINE

Jan 27, 2003

Dear Editor,

Thank you so much for replying to my story and taking the time to guide me. Yes, your magazine has touched me. I like a good steamboat read whenever I get a chance. Who doesn't? You were right. Forget the "NEW CLOTHESLINE" story. It's not right for Steamboat Magazine. Now I see that; you pointed it out to me. What was missing from that story was the Steamboating. There was nothing in my clothesline story about a steamboat. FENCER'S QUARTERLY is reading it now. Maybe they'll like it.

I am enclosing a new story which I believe captures steamboating, steamboat people, and steam in general. The name of that story is "CONJUGAL CAL". (Steaming is sprinkled throughout. In BOLD)

Thank you once again for guiding me. You're a nice lady.

Also, I would like to inquire about taking out an ad in your magazine for my business. How much is that? Thanks for the info.

Respectfully,

Ed Broth

Ed Broth

CONJUGAL CAL*
*THE STEAMBOATER

When I was a youngster my cousin Phillipe told me his Uncle Bosco used to read to him a book called "CONJUGAL CAL FROM CALICO COVE". It was about the adventures of Conjugal Cal, a prisoner with a big red moustache and thinning red hair who used to have conjugal visits while he was incarcerated. He had a girlfriend named Margareetio. Conjugal Cal was from Calico Cove which was a small town where Cal got into trouble stealing things and was sent to prison. Phillipe said he loved the little stories and they helped him fall asleep.

Years later when I was asked to write my own short stories I remembered Conjugal Cal and his many adventures in that tiny trailer on the prison grounds that Phillipe used to tell me about. I tried to contact Phillipe but I was told he had fled the United States and I was not to try and find him. His Uncle Bosco had moved on to a respectable position as a water delivery man and did not want to discuss his cousin anymore but yes, Uncle Bosco did remember the Conjugal Cal stories and he did not mind if I used them. Let me read to you one of Conjugal Cal's adventures:

USED WITH PERMISSION FROM
"CONJUGAL CAL FROM CALICO COVE."
FROM THE BOOK: It was a hot humid day at Bushy Mountain Prison in North Carolina. The sky was bright because the sun was shining. When the sun was shining the sky was usually bright. The prisoners were milling around in the exercise

yard. Some were lifting weights, some were playing dominoes with buttons, one was staggering across the yard clutching his arm, two were posing. (One had a funny little hat on.) One had fencing gear on. All the prisoners were busy on the yard. All except one. Conjugal Cal. He was in his little trailer on the prison grounds waiting for a visit from his sweetie, Margareetio. It was 8 in the morning and although a little early, it was the time that the Warden scheduled for Cal. **In the distance there was a steamboat noise. Toot! Toot!**

"I have many prisoners here besides you, Cal, that need to be serviced. They need sex like you too or else they will explode if they don't blow off a little steam. **No relation to steamboating.** Some hold their arm. I'm sorry. Next time I'll schedule you for a nooner," the Warden said to Conjugal Cal.

"That's OK, Warden, you won't hear a peep out of me. Except for later around 10:15 when I make a grunt and a bleep."

Now the Warden was busy with his fencing team. He had lined them all up to engage in a prison fencing match. There must have been 71 prisoners out there by the conjugal visit trailer all of them ready to go at it against each other with their sharp swords and mesh masks. One prisoner's name was Maestro Funches Jr. who many believed was related to the Grand Master Fencing Champeen. Oh, the fencers were having a grand time ready to engage in a grand sport on this grand sunny day.

Now many prisoners wait for that conjugal visit. That time when they can be reunited with their girlfriend or wife and enjoy themselves as before when they were free men. Not the sickness that goes on in prison today that you see on a cable show 75 times a week. Not that sickness which I can only watch 50 minutes of before I have to turn it off in disgust. (And believe me I have been disgusted many times. As many as 75 times in a week.)

Margareetio arrived at 7:30 in the morning on the bus. She had on a sparkly dress. Some of the sparkles shook off as she moved down the bus steps. She was a big woman and the dress had many sparkles. When a big woman moves sparklies fly off. She was driven to the prison in a Comfort Inn Courtesy Van. **(The steamboat was not available).** She opened the door to that tiny trailer that was near the Warden's clothesline with his prison skiivies flapping on them and Conjugal Cal had a big smile on his face. "Margareetio, give me a fat sloppy kiss," he said. "Get on over here, big woman. Save some sparkles for me." (Some more sparklies fell off as she went over to Conjugal Cal.) **He was steaming.**

The Warden kept an eye on his prisoner as they both went into that tiny trailer. Who knows what went on in there? Huh? But the Warden also kept an eye on his fencing team which was assembled by the clothesline where the Warden's undies were hanging and flapping. They were really flapping. The sky was starting to get dark. The prison fencers were really going at it fencing away. Swish! Swoosh! Swash! went their swords as they parried and swiveled about getting dangerously close to the Warden's clothesline with his underwear on it flapping away. Almost like they were waving.

Conjugal Cal yelled out from his trailer: "Hey, you wanna knock off that fencing noise out there. We're trying to have sex in here!!! **And then a Toot! Toot! was heard from the trailer. It was the two of them on their conjugal visit, not the steamboat. Toot! Toot! As Conjugal Cal emerged from that tiny trailer with a grin on his face, Master Funches Jr. nudged another prisoner—fencer and said: "That's not Conjugal Cal from Calico Cove. That's Steam-room Steve From Steamboat Springs."**

The other prisoner's name was Tony. Tony Smudge. "Are you sure?" said Tony as he adjusted his fencing tights? (They creep up in the back when you squat)

"Sure as I'm standin' here pokin' at you with my twangy long sword. I know Steamroom Steve From Steamboat Springs like the back of my hand. Even if it has a bandaid on it.

"Are you sure, sure, sure?" said Tony Smudge.

"I'm double sure, triple sure, and quadruple sure sure sure," bellowed Master Funches Jr. as he parried and wooshed with his fencing sword. "Steamroom Steve was the captain of a steam-room on a steamboat. He wore a yachting cap and stayed outside the steamroom as men took a stream on that boat. Always around alot of men sweating in towels."

"My, my, my" said Tony Smudge. Isn't that something?"

"Yep. He's a riverboat gambler, card shark, pool hustler, telemarketer, impostor. Went to jail for stealing a bag of bananas. Got 6 years. So far he's had 53 conjugal visits. Been in prison since November. Passed himself off as Conjugal Cal from Calico Cove. Hid the bananas someplace. That's him

emerging from that sex trailer, steamin' himself up with Margareetio and her sparklies fallin' off. 'Nuff said?"

"You sure he's not Sassy Sandy From Saggy Harbor?" said Tony Smudge to Master Funches Jr. "I mean he sure looks like Sassy Sandy From Saggy Harbor."

"Hell no! I saw his picture in a steamboat magazine which is published bi-annually, $19.00 per year, $32.00 in Canada. And you know what? I'm gonna challenge him." And so they went up to the red moustached man who had just had some pleasure—this Master Funches Jr. and this Tony—and they approached him flat out: "On guard, Monsieur Steamroom Steve from Steamboat Springs. If that is indeed who you are. Touche." As they squatted in their tights and funny masks and stuck their sword in his face.

And Conjugal Cal said, "You got the wrong guy! "I'm Conjugal Cal from Calico Cove not Steamroom Steve From Steamboat Springs. And I'm certainly not Sassy Sandy From Saggy Harbor."

The Warden yelled out: "What are you three cons babbling about? Huh? I'm perturbed." All the while the warden fenced by his clothesline as his undies flapped and waved in the dark sky. (He also put some shorty pajamas up.) "We got to get the fencing team ready for the big tournament with Sing Sing. Forget about another man's pleasures. Just squat some more with your swords and dance around at each other. I'll keep points."

NOTE TO READER: Now was the time when I was a lad that Phillipe told me he drifted off to sleep and Uncle Bosco would say "You missed a lot of the story." And sleepy Phillipe would say, "What happened?" Phillipe said he was tired for many years and never really got much past this part that I just read to you. Once he said he made it to a few pages more to a viscous argument between Margareetio and Conjugal Cal where she said "I won't do that" and "That's disgusting" and "Phooey." But that was it. His Uncle Bosco never read further to little Phillipe from that book.

The Conjugal Cal books were published in 64 languages and became best sellers in Germany. Eventually they were made into a movie there with Tom Cruise turning down the part of Conjugal Cal. In my letters to Tom Cruise (there were 12 of them) I suggested that he made a bad career move by not playing Conjugal Cal. After all they were both frisky people. And the books were big sellers. To date he has not answered me.

MAMMA

Mamma was a hard working woman. She took care of our family. There were 10 of us. Me and 9 other people. Mamma's full name was LeeLee Finchman Broth. A proud name for a proud Lilliputian woman. (A sturdy woman)

Mamma worked as a saleslady at "THE BEDWETTERS STORE". They were part of a chain. This particular store was located in the Crestview Mall. The Crestview Mall was in Cumberland Valley (not Cumberland County!) Off Cumberland Valley Boulevard. It was in the Tri Area, Triad, Tri Region section of town. "The Bedwetter's Store" had everything for the bedwetter. From rubber sheets to aluminum pans. From dribble cups to bowls. From mystic music to help you wet your bed to reading material to aid you when you're wetting your bed. Mamma was their best saleslady selling about 22 rubber sheets a week. They also stocked fungal vests to sleep in. Plus they had a nice selection of James Brown music to help you urinate. It was proven that James Brown was the most requested music for urination problems. I had written to James Brown 11 times to tell him this but to date I have not heard back.

Our neighbor Carmo said that he had been wetting the bed for 41 years and he shopped at "The Bedwetters Store" for 30 years and would only let my mother wait on him. He told me that he sometimes got up in the middle of the night, his bed soaken with urine, and that he had to change the rubber sheet and remove the soiled and urine soaked mattress cover, and stop his James Brown song from playing, and he always thought of my mother. I didn't really know how to take that except to smile at Carmo and thank him for what I guess was a compliment. Then I would come home and tell Mamma about Carmo's "compliment" and Mamma would cringe. But she wouldn't say anything bad about Carmo. Mamma used to say "If you can't say anything nice about a person then find someone else who can't say anything nice about that person and agree with them."

There were two bedding stores in Cumberland County. "The Bedwetters Store" and "LEE HARVEY OSWALD MATTRESS SHOP". Three brothers named Lee, Harvey, and Oswald started that store. Two of the brothers went to school with a brother and sister, Jack and Ruby. They were friends with three brothers named James, Earl, and Ray who lived next door to two other brothers and their dog: Martin, Luther, and King. (This never got confusing)

Lee, Harvey, and Oswald had wanted to go into business together for a long, long time and in November of 1963 they realized this was the best time. They finally opened the mattress shop. They got a lot of looky loos at that store, a lot of passerbys, many browsers, not too many shoppers. But if you wet the bed then you definitely *shopped* at Mamma's store. The other store was mostly people bouncing on mattresses, plumping up pillows, squishing bedding, sniffing demo pillows, belching up olives, shining their shoes on comforters. (I vowed to get into a business with a catchy name like that. Years later I had a chance to open SAUNA SAM which sold saunas but the SON OF SAM creep claimed the name was too close. To my chagrin)

Well, wouldn't you know it but a new store opened in the Crestview Mall that winter. RICHARD SPECKS—THE EYEGLASS STORE. I had my broken eyeglasses repaired there and Carlton Richard was the optometrist. "Better like this? Or better this way?" he said to me as he offered me a toasted or un-toasted bagel one morning. That was the one thing that drove me crazy about Carlton Richard.

Everything was always 'Better like this? Or better like this' no matter what he was showing me—His shirt out of his pants or in. His hair combed with a part or without. "Better now? Or better like this?" he would say as he combed his hair over. "Better this way? Or better now?" he said as he showed me a picture on the wall that was hung high then hung lower. Once he showed me a bougar in his nostril. "Better like this or better this way?" As I looked at his nostril with a green thingamigiggy in it.

There was a sign on his wall that read: "Free Tint With Every 2nd Pair." I said "I'm glad you had an "N" in there. If the N ever falls off your sign I'm gonna demand my free tint less the N." Today Carlton Speck walks around with his shirt half out and sea dribble in his ear. The eyeglass shop is closed and a petting zoo is in its place. At the Crestview Mall. I have not been back.

Mamma was a hard worker like I said. Frank Tint is no good. I despise him. (I have mentioned him in the past)

FINO

DADDY WAS A BEDWETTER

Daddy wet the bed until he was 56. The last three years he stood up on the side to do it. He was fully awake yet he could not control himself. Had we had Zoloc back then it may have helped. (Side effects include itchy scalp, abdominal cramps, shouting at people named Lou.)

Daddy met Mamma at "The Bedwetters Store" and that's where they held their wedding reception. They were going to hold it at the most elegant restaurant in town—"THE CHEF'S DIABETIC FOOT"—but the Chef wouldn't let Daddy in anymore after years of stealing from his restaurant. So "The Bedwetters Store" hosted the wedding. The "Chef's Diabetic Foot" was really the place to hold the wedding. It was THE place to see and be seen. The Chef had a swollen and red foot for many years. People told the Chef to have his blotchy leg looked at but he always shrugged it off with a cavalier nod and an unceremonious languor.

The restaurant was very elegant. Food was brought to the table in a chafing dish that was in the shape of a disfigured foot. "Forget pirate themes and lobster netting," said the Chef. "This place is unique." And I must say their pancakes on a rope were indeed tasty.

Now people tried to reason with the Chef that the wedding really should be held in a restaurant and not in a bedding store but he did not like Daddy. It was as simple as that. The months went by and the Chef's condition worsened. People said you really ought to have that turgid foot looked at but the Chef just shrugged it off with a colloquial recognition and an unconstrained lassitude. Right before the wedding, the restaurant closed for a month and when it reopened it had a new name: "THE CHEF'S ARTIFICIAL LEG".

What a beautiful event! Daddy and Mamma said their
vows under a rubber sheet canopy. Music was played. A
cat meowed. Everyone clapped along with everyone else
when they played Glen Campbell's song "Stomach Full Of
Fudge".

Now "The Chef's Artificial Leg Restaurant" I must say
here was one of the finest seafood establishments in
Cumberland County. Their best seller was an artificial leg
stuffed with crabmeat that is dee-licious. It's a nice size
serving. Also their skunk on a skewer is a classic.
Chunks of skunk with bell peppers and onions and toma-
toes on a skewer. And if you still have a sweet tooth—try
their Frog Newtons. "We Leave The Hand Suctions On" is
their motto."

The Bedwetters Store really held a gala soiree that
night. Glen Campbell music streamed from the speakers.
(I personally liked "Itches For My Lady".) Daddy and the
Chef were on really bad terms now. The hatred had
reached a fever. Daddy just shrugged it off and called the
Chef an ugly little gimp of a toad of a loser of a man.
"But I like his soup, Daddy said."

The months went by and the Chef's condition worsened. He closed his restaurant for a while when he was
in the hospital and when it reopened it had a new name:
"THE CHEF'S STUMP". I must say that The Chef's Stump
Restaurant was a pretty darn good restaurant. The food
was very elegant and the Chef made sure to prepare
your meal with the finest ingredients. It quickly caught
on to be Cumberland's finest. I personally liked the Pita
Pan which was a pita dish in a pan that resembled the
pixie in the Captain Hook movie.

Who would have thought they would have made up.
Huh? But they did! It was really special to see the Chef
and Daddy make up. Forget their problems and become
friends again. Later on when the Chef lost his other leg

and both his arms due to a clam chowder accident, Daddy helped him with a singles ad to attract a woman. The first line of the ad read:

SENSITIVE TORSO. TURN ME OVER. I GET WIGGLY.

The Chef met a nice woman named Beth Finkelstein who he eventually married and Daddy, believe it or not, was best man. Beth was a real estate agent in Cumberland and loved the Chef even though he was a half stumped torso with a snotty disposition. His red beard was also annoying to watch him eat tartar sauce and take a drink of water and balance himself on the stove. Beth eventually left the Chef for another man with no legs and no arms. That eventually destroyed him. He was not even 1/4th of a man then.

Daddy helped the Chef get back on his makeshift feet again and meet a new woman. He helped him with his new singles ad. "First," he told the Chef, "Is to lose your email address DIAPERFULL@NETSCAPE. It's a bad image. Get a new email address," Daddy told him. The first line of the new singles ad read:

SEEKING FRESH BULLSHIT

The Chef received a reply from a woman who wrote in her ad that she was a DWF. The Chef thought it was a Divorced White Female. It was a dwarf. Her name was Arlene Markowitz who worked as a Jewelry saleslady and she sold the Chef some nice spangly bracelets. (Which he wore on his head)

Eventually she too ran off on him for a corpse leaving the Chef once again to compose a new singles ad. He asked my Daddy for help and the first line of the ad read:

NO MORE JEWISH WOMEN

The Chef met a nice woman from Singapore and I understand they settled down and had a ton of kids. He eventually went back into the restaurant business opening up "THE CHEF'S NECK" restaurant. (in Cumberland County). The Chef can be reached at his current email address: FAGGY@HOTMAIL

BROKEN GARAGE DOOR

My garage door was broken today. It would not open. Today is November 30, 2002. The day before my rent is due. So it came at a bad time. It could be expensive. It was the spring in the top of the door. And me being a 4 foot 9 inch man around 285 pounds with boils, I could not reach it. Even if I put on my boot with the big heel. (The one I wear to meet girls) That's how I met Sandee. I was wearing the boot with the big heel and she was attracted to me. (Or it.) I called "AAAAAB GARAGE DOOR REPAIRS" in the Yellow Pages. I called them because they were listed second. I had trouble with another garage door company before—"AAAAAABB Garage Door Repairs"—and did not want to use them again.

The garage door repairman came and I showed him the problem. I told him that the door would not open all the way. He looked at it from all angles. Underneath, sideways, over the top, he compared it to a picture in his truck. I saw another picture under that picture of a dog with a sailor hat on. The garage door repairman was a smelly man, full of grease and with a torn shirt. His name on his shirt was "Garbazian". He had many stains on his clothes. One stain, I think, was from some kind of jelly. It could have been grape. But then again it could have been blueberry. I am usually good at identifying jelly stains but this one had me wondering. I was dying to know but I did not want to ask him. Who was I to ask a repairman what kind of jelly stain he had? Huh? I think he was foreign. But he could have been from Glendale. There are many Garbazians there. I know. I have looked in the phone book and seen thirty five pages of Garbazians in there.

I asked this garage door repairman if he had ever read the kids book "MARIO THE LACTATING ZEBRA"? This is a story of a zebra with 8 teats going all at once like pistons in a car. He said he had an Uncle that used to read it to him as a child and he would fall asleep. I made a note of this for recall later. He was working on the door for an hour, really getting into it. He was really into this spring. I mean he was working it like a rib at a Sizzler. At one point the garage door lifted him up and he was on the edge of the door in the air going up and down haywire in my smelly garage. He said "I'm in trouble. Help me. The garage door is going fast and it could kill me." I told him that I had seen that before in an Urban Cowboy lounge I used to frequent. I was not impressed then nor was I impressed now. So he could ride my garage door? So what? If a fake bull did not impress me than why would a garage door? Huh?

I ignored him and watched him go up and down on my moving garage door rapidly. Had I been an immature 12 year old I would have pointed at him and burst out laughing going "Look at the funny man ready to fall off on my hard concrete floor."

"Help me," he said, "I need help."

"Help you? Excuse but I need you to help *me.* That is why I called *you.* To help *me,*" I said. "That's why I needed you here to fix the door. It is broken." He finally fell off but he was not hurt. Instead, he got up and resumed his working on my garage door. I noticed a stain on the back of his pants. I think it was mango. But it could have been peach. I am usually good at identifying stains on the back of pants but this one had me wondering. He said "Come closer, I want to show you this spring." I moved in to look at the spring when he said "I want to hug you. I find you so attractive that I must hug you. Hug me and I will hug you back." He grabbed for me. I said, "Please, Mister, I just want to get my garage door fixed, I don't want to be hugged."

He said, "I need you. I need to hug you. I want to hug you as the garage door opens and closes. Maybe a squeeze too." I pushed him away and said "Please, just fix my garage door and that's all I want. I don't want to be hugged OR squeezed. And I believe your jelly stain is grape!" (That's how indignant I was; it just blurted out. Some times we do things in the world that we are ashamed of. This was NOT one of them. He was after me. I just needed a garage spring fixed. What is it with these repair people?) I did not mention the mango stain on his pants. Why should I? Huh? (It could have been peach.)

We had small idle chat for a while; it was uncomfortable like when you get turned down at a bar from a busty German woman. Except this was a smelly garage door repairman. I guess busty German women and smelly garage door repairmen are all alike. I told him so. He understood; I tasted a Fudge Graham I had eaten a few days earlier. Now was the time it came up.

To continue my story: Garbazian, the garage door repairman, finished fixing my garage door in silence. When he was finished I paid the bill and he gave me the broken spring. He showed me where it had worn down. He said, "Here, this is where it has worn down." I realized I was looking at a worn down spring. So what? What did I care? Why did I have to look at this? What was the purpose? To see a worn down spring? I told him so. I paid him in dimes. He drove away in his truck. He fixed my garage door and now it opens and closes properly. I WILL NOT call this company again. I cannot recommend them, this AAAAAB Garage Doors. Next time I will call ABABABA Garage Doors. They are fourteen down in the Yellow Pages, but worth it.

I put my boot with the big heel away. I was not impressed with this Garbazian. The one on page 137 of the Glendale phone book. Phooey.

FINITIO

29 March 2004

Mr. Ed Broth
10153 1/2 Riverside Dr., #241
Toluca Lake, CA   91602

Dear Ed,

Thank you for submitting your work(s):

"Broken Garage Door"

for publication in the North American Voice of Fatima. I regret to inform you that these submissions will not meet our publishing needs. I encourage you to submit other material for consideration. May God bless you.

Yours in Jesus,

Rev.
Rev.
Editor

tricycle
THE BUDDHIST REVIEW

May 13, 2004

Dear Ed:

Thank you for your recent submission, "Broken Garage Door." Your essay was given careful consideration by the *Tricycle* editorial staff. Unfortunately, it does not relate sufficiently to Buddhism for us to consider it for publication in the magazine.

Sorry not to have better news, but I appreciate your having thought of *Tricycle* and wish you much success in placing your work elsewhere.

Best wishes,

Editorial Assistant
Tricycle: The Buddhist Review

HIGH SCHOOL DAYS

I had gone to Cumberland High. And I was an OK student. I studied and tried hard. But it was tough for me. For instance, I knew I would fail Spanish when I was failing English. But I tried to make something of myself and be the best I could. I didn't want to grow up to be a restaurant manager like my Daddy. I wanted more. Cumberland High back then was the only high school in Cumberland County. They had our school and Cumberland Elementary School. We played Cumberland Elementary School 41 times in team sports. Then we just got sick of it. Sick of their cheers and their school colors and everything about them. Our record against them was 8-31-2. I have to admit even though they were much smaller and younger then us they were good. (We were sick of them)

I never really played sports in high school. I was not a good athlete, let's face it. (Even though I was strapping and had good lats.) I was not good in the usual high school sports like the Javelin Toss or the Hammer Throw. But I did excel in the Groin Pull. Our whole school was pretty bad in sports. Our football team mascot was a goldfish that floated to the top of the bowl.

After high school I worked at "THE PIMPLY LATINO MENS SHOP". This was where all the kids got their clothes and I was a stock boy and measured shirts. I was OK at it. I always thought the store was way too big for just a clothing store. The Pimply Latino closed soon after I graduated and today it is an airport. Where I once put out Ban-lons there are now Boeing 747s. I was in there recently browsing for a few shirts when I noticed a lot of planes. That's how I found out.

I had a girlfriend in High School. Her name was Teenie. Which was not our dog. I know our dog and my girl-

friend had the same name which was some confusion but
Teenie was a full big strapping woman maybe 256
pounds over 5'11 and Teenie was our pet Chihuahua
who weighed maybe 16. Teenie was my girlfriend's
name. That was her real name. Southern women had
names like that when I was growing up in Cumberland
County. Teenie and Shereee and Lisa Lee. I once knew a
girl named April Mae June. She worked at the bakery
and she was fast with twine.

Teenie & Teenie had the same spelling and Daddy
would say "Why don't you just spell the dog's name different?" And I said, "They still sound the same, Daddy. I
don't need to write the dog's name down unless I carry
my girlfriend into the vet by mistake." Daddy barely
heard me. He just stood there and watered his eyes then
barked out: I NEED A WHITE WOMAN!! And then collapsed; went down in three stages like a cheap lawn
chair.

Sometimes I would stand outside and Yell "Teenie!!"
And my girlfriend would come runnin'. There was some
confusion when I told Mamma that Teenie went doo doo
on the carpet and she yelled at my girlfriend for an hour.
Teenie burst into tears and ran all the way home. (She

Teenie - Dog

Teenie - girlfriend

did not do the doo doo. I stuck up for her. But because she ONCE did a doo doo on the carpet, my argument meant nothing.)

Teenie loved to lick me. She licked me real good all over. She would lay on her back and let me kiss her all over. Teenie was somethin'. Daddy once came in to the room when Teenie was on the couch lickin' me. He said "You just sit there all day rubbin' her don't you? Maybe if you got off the couch and chased Teenie away you would get something done." I never did. I loved Teenie, I could never do that. One day Teenie just ran away. I got a letter from her and she said she missed me and was coming home if I didn't spend so much time with the dog.

Teenie lived in the Cumberland Valley which was in Cumberland County but it had it's own newspaper: The Cumberland Daily and our newspaper was The Cumberland Daily Express. So there was more confusion when I asked Teenie to go fetch the paper.

Our song in high school was Mickey Goolley's "Bladder Full Of Walnuts". Teenie and I slow danced to that song over a hundred times. The first time we made out—(In the back of "The Pimply Latino Mens Shop")—"Bladder Full of Walnuts" was playing. I got Teenie's shirt off just as Mickey Goolley sang: 'She had a bladder full of walnuts. I had a pocketful of cash. She had a bladder full of pistachios. I caught you pecan through her shirt. And If I cash-ew, you're in trouble. She was nuts about meeeee!'

That was our favorite song. I heard years later that Mickey Goolley left the music business and became a robot salesman in Lubbock, Texas. I had hoped not because he was a great singer and "Bladder Full Of Walnuts" is a song I still ask for at the car wash. (If they have the album).

Teenie's stepfather, Gene, worked at "FAT MAN CLAPPING HAIRCUTTERS". His name was Gene Gassy and he was really skinny. Maybe 110 pounds and 6 foot. He had a big Adams apple and thinning hair (what was left of it) and blotchy skin. But a nice blotch. Some blotchy skin is pasty. His was not. Everyone said he looked like Warren Beatty. Handsome man. The ladies liked him. He was a barber and that's how he supported his family.

"Fat Man Clapping Haircutters" was a chain that had just opened a branch in the Mall. In the corner of the barbershop was a mechanical Fat Man that stood there and clapped over and over while you got your hair cut. After a while I guess you could get used to it. But I was tired of it after 20 minutes. Teenie's stepfather wore a fecal vest to work in case anybody threw stuff at him. But you could regulate the clapping to go slower or faster. I have to admit the slower clapping got on my nerves. Mickey Goolley fixed it once.

That was my High School reminisces growing up.

Muzzle Blasts

Official Publication of the National Muzzle Loading Rifle Association

January 13, 2002

Ed Broth
10153½ Riverside Drive
#241
Toluca Lake, CA 91602

Dear Mr. Broth,

       Thanks for writing. I am glad you enjoy our magazine, however your article can not be used in *Muzzle Blasts* because it doesn't concern muzzleloading. You are welcome to write another article and submit it. I have enclosed our writer's guidelines to help you tailor future articles to our publication.

Best Wishes,

Melinda Baxter
Muzzle Blasts Secretary

Enclosures

P.O. BOX 67/STATE ROUTE 62   FRIENDSHIP, INDIANA 47021   TEL (812) 667-5131
FAX (812) 667-5137   EMAIL MBLASTMAG@SEIDATA.COM

Ed Broth
10153 ½ Riverside Dr.
#241
Toluca Lake, CA 91602

Melinda Baxter
Editor, MUZZLE BLASTS MAGAZINE
Official Publication Of the National Muzzle Loading Assoc.
P.O. Box 67/State Route 62
Friendship, Indiana 47021

Jan 18, 2003

Dear Editor Baxter,

Thank you for reading my story: "HIGH SCHOOL DAYS". I am glad
you like it. AND encouraged that you encourage me. Yes, I now see
that my story does not have anything to do with muzzleloading.
Having re-read my story I see that more clearly now.
    Perhaps I sent you the wrong story. Enclosed is my new story
and the muzzleloading references you desire. Thank you for
pointing this out to me. It is a better story now. I have put the new
muzzleloading additions in **BOLD & UNDERLINED** and fuzzed out
the story you read before so you can read the revised story more
efficiently.

With Respect,

Ed Broth

Ed Broth

HIGH SCHOOL DAYS (WITH A LOT OF OF MUZZLE BLASTING)

I had gone to Cumberland High. And I was an OK student. I studied and tried hard. But it was tough for me. For instance, I knew I would fail Spanish when I was failing English. But I tried to make something of myself and be the best I could. I didn't want to grow up to be a restaurant manager like my Daddy. I wanted more. Cumberland High back then was the only high school in Cumberland County. They had our school and Cumberland Elementary School. We played Cumberland Elementary School 41 times in team sports. Then we just got sick of it. Sick of their cheers and their school colors and everything about them. Our record against them was 8-31-2. I have to admit even though they were much smaller and younger then us they were good. (We were sick of them)

I never really played sports in high school. I was not a good athlete, let's face it. (Even though I was strapping and had good lats.) I was not good in the usual high school sports like the Javelin Toss or the Hammer Throw. But I did excel in the Groin Pull. Our whole school was pretty bad in sports. Our football team mascot was a goldfish that floated to the top of the bowl.

After high school I worked at "THE PIMPLY LATINO MENS SHOP". This was where all the kids got their clothes and I was a stock boy and measured shirts. I was OK at it. I always thought the store was way too big for just a clothing store. The Pimply Latino closed soon after I graduated and today it is an airport. Where I once put out Ban-lons there are now Boeing 747s. I was in there recently browsing for a few shirts when I noticed a lot of planes. That's how I found out.

I had a girlfriend in High School. Her name was Teenie. Which was not our dog. I know our dog and my girlfriend had the same name which was some confusion but
Teenie was a full big strapping woman maybe 256
pounds over 5'11 and Teenie was our pet Chihuahua
who weighed maybe 16. Teenie was my girlfriend's
name. That was her real name. Southern women had
names like that when I was growing up in Cumberland
County. Teenie and Shereee and Lisa Lee. I once knew a
girl named April Mae June. She worked at the bakery
and she was fast with twine.

**Teenie took a shot to the stomach once with a muzzle
blast. Whooee! What a mess! But she was OK thanks to
quick thinking from a neighbor. Later the neighbor
cleaned up the mess. (From the dog who got scared.)**

Teenie & Teenie had the same spelling and Daddy
would say "Why don't you just spell the dog's name different?" And I said, "They still sound the same, Daddy. I
don't need to write the dog's name down unless I carry
my girlfriend into the vet by mistake."

Daddy barely heard me. He just stood there and
watered his eyes then barked out: I NEED A WHITE
WOMAN!! And then collapsed; went down in three stages
like a cheap lawn chair.

Teenie - girl friend

Teenie - Dog

Sometimes I would stand outside and Yell "Teenie!!" And my girlfriend would come runnin'. There was some confusion when I told Mamma that Teenie went doo doo on the carpet and she yelled at my girlfriend for an hour. Teenie burst into tears and ran all the way home. (She did not do the doo doo. I stuck up for her. But because she ONCE did a doo doo on the carpet, my argument meant nothing.

Teenie loved to lick me. She licked me real good all over. She would lay on her back and let me kiss her all over. Teenie was somethin'. Daddy once came in to the room when Teenie was on the couch lickin' me. He said "You just sit there all day rubbin' her don't you? Maybe if you got off the couch and chased Teenie away you would get something done." I never did. I loved Teenie, I could never do that. One day Teenie just ran away. I got a letter from her and she said she missed me and was coming home if I didn't spend so much time with the dog.

I once bought a long rifle at the Mall. And the sales-man said "You better know how to muzzle clean that thing. And I wouldn't be waving it around; sticking it up somebody's shorties." I called him Otto and yelled out a shrimp dish.

Teenie lived in the Cumberland Valley which was in Cumberland County but it had it's own newspaper: The Cumberland Daily and our newspaper was The Cumberland Daily Express. So there was more confusion when I asked Teenie to go fetch the paper.

Our song in high school was Mickey Goolley's "Bladder Full Of Walnuts". Teenie and I slow danced to that song over a hundred times. The first time we made out— (In the back of "The Pimply Latino Mens Shop")—"Bladder Full of Walnuts" was playing. I got Teenie's shirt off just as Mickey Goolley sang: 'She had a bladder full of walnuts. I had a pocketful of cash. She had a bladder full of pistachios. I caught you pecan through her shirt. And if I cash-ew, you're in trouble. She was nuts about meeeee!' That was our favorite song. I heard years later that Mickey Goolley left the music business and became a robot salesman in Lubbock, Texas. I had hoped not because he was a great singer and "Bladder Full Of Walnuts" is a song I still ask for at the car wash. (If they have the album).

Teenie's stepfather, Gene, worked at "FAT MAN CLAPPING HAIRCUTTERS". His name was Gene Gassy and he was really skinny. Maybe 110 pounds and 6 foot. He had a big Adams apple and thinning hair (what was left of it) and blotchy skin. But a nice blotch. Some blotchy skin is pasty. His was not. Everyone said he looked like Warren Beatty. Handsome man. The ladies liked him. He was a barber and that's how he supported his family.

"Fat Man Clapping Haircutters" was a chain that had just opened a branch in the Mall. In the corner of the barbershop was a mechanical Fat Man that stood there and clapped over and over while you got your hair cut. After a while I guess you could get used to it. But I was tired of it after 20 minutes. Teenie's stepfather wore a fecal vest to work in case anybody threw stuff at him. But you could regulate the clapping to go slower or faster. I have to admit the slower clapping got on my nerves. Mickey Goolley fixed it once.

I got a muzzle for Teenie. Daddy told me to. The salesman at the pet store's name was Hector Gassy. No realtion to Gene Gassy, her stepfather.

That was my High School reminisces growing up.

Muzzle Blasts

Official Publication of the National Muzzle Loading Rifle Association

Jan. 27, 2003

Ed Broth
10153 ½ Riverside Dr.
#241
Toluca Lake,
CA 91602

Dear Ed:

It was nice of you to amend your manuscript submission to include reference to muzzleloading, but unfortunately I must return it to you once again, and once and for all. Perhaps you are not familiar with *Muzzle Blasts*, and I need to stress that it is dedicated to competitive shooting, hunting, and gunsmithing with muzzleloaders. The type of material you have submitted to us simply does not meet our editorial needs. We are interested in technical and "how-to" articles pertaining to that specific type of firearm. Inserting a couple of passing references to the field does not make an otherwise unqualified article acceptable for publication. Our writers have years of experience dealing with the practical matters of shooting muzzleloaders, and their technical expertise is what our readers expect.

You may have success finding some other publication that is interested in your manuscript, but it is not appropriate material for *Muzzle Blasts*. Good luck.

Sincerely,

Eric A. Bye, Editor

P.O. BOX 67/STATE ROUTE 62 FRIENDSHIP, INDIANA 47021 TEL (812) 667-5131
FAX (812) 667-5137 EMAIL MBLASTMAG@SEIDATA.COM

ED BROTH
10153 ½ Riverside Dr.
#241
Toluca Lake, CA 91602

Editor Eric A. Bye
MUZZLE BLASTS MAGAZINE
Official Publication of the
Nat'l Muzzle Loading Rifle Assoc.
PO Box 67/State Route 62
Friendship, Indiana 47021

Feb 2, 03

Dear Editor Mr. Bye,

Thank you for replying to my fixed up story: "HIGH SCHOOL
DAYS." Forget that story. Just forget it. It is not right for Muzzle
Blasts Magazine. I forced it in. I can see it now. After reading it I
can see you were correct. There is nothing in that story in any
way shape or form about competitive shooting, hunting, and
gunsmithing with muzzleloaders per your letter. (Although I
thought there was.) Nor is there anything in there regarding
technical and "how to" do anything pertaining to any kind of
firearms. It is simply not right for your magazine. I see that now.

However, I am submitting a new story which I think captures
what your readers are seeking. I know what you want now. I hope
this story meets your requirements. Let's get me in your
magazine! I am ready!

Also, I was thinking . . . I would like to advertise in your
magazine for my business. I like your magazine and think an ad in
there would be good for me. How much?

Sincerely,

Ed Broth

Ed Broth

DADDY WAS A MUZZLE BLASTER

I was born in Cumberland County. Daddy was a muzzle blaster. Let me just tell you that. His daddy before him was a muzzle blaster. And his daddy's daddy was a muzzle blaster. Their daddy's were all muzzle blasters. Every man in my family was a muzzle blaster. They just weren't right. (To have this many muzzle blasters) This had gone back in my family to the year 1612. We were riddled with muzzle blasting. Then it was a normal father, 2 chubby men, a big guy named Roy, then a midsize man about 160 pounds, then in 1217 another muzzle blaster guy, then there were three more muzzle blasters, another normal guy (we think—could have been a muzzle blaster), a giant, and then a muzzle blaster again. (I think his name was Perry).

I am not a muzzle blaster. I am a fencer.

I have always enjoyed fencing. Fencing is a wonderful sport. I really like fencing, its people, its tournaments, and its magazines. However this story is about muzzle blasting. Not fencing. I have written enough fencing stories. Muzzle Blasting is really the way to go.

Daddy used to take me muzzle blasting. We'd go out into the woods and hunt with our long shotguns. (There was a muzzle on the end). One day Daddy took a shot with his shotgun at what he thought was a buffalo. And a buffalo cub. But it was really Teenie and Teenie. They just all looked alike—that buffalo, the baby buffalo, my girlfriend and our dog. It was sad but it was true. "I didn't know it was your girlfriend and your dog," said Daddy. "I thought they were buffaloes. Your girlfriend is huge, she needs to go on a diet. If I thought she was a buffalo then she is just getting way too big."

"Well," I said, "Lets not bring up the weight of another

TEENIE-DOG   Teenie - Girlfriend   BUFFALO   BUFFALO Jr.

person now. We're hunting. We're muzzle loading, muzzle blasting, we're doing things with shotguns and muzzling now not castigating another individual because they have a piece of pastry or two." (And some burgers). He said he was sorry. But I didn't believe him. I tasted a Licorice Nib I had been snacking on.

Daddy was outfitted like a Revolutionary War soldier: buckskin chaps, coonskin cap, lots of fringey things flapping on him. He had a big long rifle with a muzzle on the end. He poked that rifle around and almost got me in the shorties. (But I backed away). Daddy yelled "Charge!" then shot a muzzle ball at the buffalo. But it was just Teenie eating ice cream by a tree. She yelled out "I'm eating ice cream here. Watch out with that damn muzzle rifle, you fool!"

Daddy yelled back: "I thought it looked stupid to see a buffalo eating ice cream!"

Teenie yelled back "Is there any more ice cream?"

Daddy yelled back "I dunno, did you eat it all?" And that's the way it went all afternoon. Daddy in his stretchy Revolutionary War outfit shooting muzzle balls at my girlfriend who was eating ice cream cones by a tree. We bagged nothing. The dog got sick from some woodsy berries and dribbled in the car.

I forgot to mention: Daddy told us he was dedicated to competitive shooting, hunting, and gunsmithing with muzzleloaders. He was also interested in technical and "how to" articles. When we went hunting he told us that. He said he read it somewhere but he couldn't remember where. Daddy was a muzzleloader through and through. Sure he wet the bed but that didn't stop him from muzzleloading. Mamma knew this. She married a a muzzle loadin' bedwetter.

We drove home that night and Teenie's stepfather, Gene, was just getting home from work at the "Fat Man Clapping Haircutters". His vest looked like it was from San Quentin when prisoners throw their stuff at the guards. But it must have been from the damn fat man robot clapping in the corner of the barbershop that annoyed the people getting their haircuts. It always spewed off debris at people. He told me Mickey Goolley had fixed it so it didn't clap so fast but now it clapped really slow and that annoyed the people more. "Where you been?" he said.

"We were muzzleblasting and we almost shot Teenie".

"Which one?" he asked.

"Does it make a difference?" I asked him.

"Not really, he said, just curious, except one of them Teenies is my daughter."

"Which one?" I said.

He said "The big heavy girl. Which one did you think?"

I honestly did not know how to answer him. So I said "Just because a person has an extra burger or two (and some pastry) doesn't mean you should refer to them as heavy. You can call them portly or husky or stout or even plump or fleshy but heavy is derogatory to a jumbo person."

He said "Tell her to lay off the burgers and maybe she wouldn't get shot at. She looks like a buffalo."

I said, "Well, you're a fine one, aren't you?" I love muzzle blasting!

Muzzle Blasts

Official Publication of the National Muzzle Loading Rifle Association

February 7, 2003

Ed Broth
10153 ½ Riverside Drive
#241
Toluca Lake, CA 91602

Dear Mr. Broth,

We have received your article "Daddy Was a Muzzle Blaster." Unfortunately we are unable to use your article in any current issue of *Muzzle Blasts*, therefore I am returning your article to you. Also enclosed is an ad rate card should you chose to advertise with us.

Thank you for your submission, if you have any questions or comments please feel free to contact us.

Sincerely,

Melinda Baxter
Muzzle Blasts Secretary

P.O. BOX 67/STATE ROUTE 62 FRIENDSHIP, INDIANA 47021 TEL (812) 667-5131
FAX (812) 667-5137 EMAIL MBLASTMAG@SEIDATA.COM

Stories of Dignity and Esteem

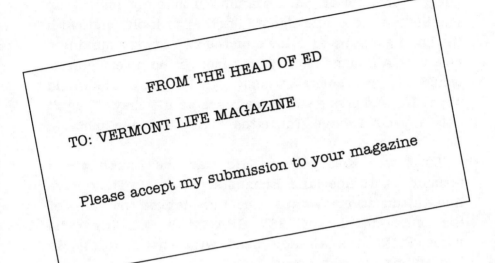

FROM THE HEAD OF ED

TO: VERMONT LIFE MAGAZINE

Please accept my submission to your magazine

TOURETTES SIGN LANGUAGE

My neighbor Kelsey Pinto was recently diagnosed with TOURETTES SIGN LANGUAGE. This is a disease for people who have Tourettes Syndrome but cannot speak. Instead they make involuntary obscene gestures at people. They shoot someone the finger, give them the bird, brush the hand under the chin, grab their crotch with a "Here's your obscene sign right here, Pal" movement, bend over and spread their buttocks at you. Things like that. Now as we all know, Tourettes Syndrome is the disease where one can't help barking out obscenities. These people can't bark out anything because they can't talk; but they still have the disease so they have to make obscene signs at people to let them know they're cursing.

Kelsey Pinto had this disease. He was a mute. Kelsey would stand on his porch and make involuntary obscene signs to passerbys. Many a times Mamma caught a few of his rude "remarks." He would always get very apologetic and blush then try and have a normal sign lan-

guage conversation with Mamma ultimately ending up
making more obscene signs: Like the "jerk off" sign with
the hand going up and down or the two fingers making a
hole with another finger going through the hole. Then he
would say he's sorry through sign language: He would
shrug his shoulders with a sad face as if to say, "I can't
help myself I have Tourettes Sign Language disease.
Bear with me."

That was Kelsey Pinto. He was the fourth grade
teacher at Cumberland Elementary School. They gave
him an educational award once and changed the name of
the school to the KELSEY GRAMMAR SCHOOL. (The
name Pinto was already used with the College). He
showed me his rash once.

Now I had never seen or heard this kind of language
before. The closest I came to any filth like this is when a
one man show came to town: "HAL HOLBROOK AS
HARRY TRUMAN SLAMMING THE CAR DOOR ON HIS
FINGER".

Hal Holbrook played Harry Truman—our God fearing;
Christian worshiping, highly moral President of the
United States who closed the car door on his finger resulting in his letting out a stream of obscenities. Here are a
few lines from the play I remember when my parents
took me to see it at the Cumberland County Religious Regional Theater one Christmas.* (SEE FOOTNOTE)

FROM THE PLAY:

"Now being President is a pretty darn good thing. I
remember one particular day while I was in the White
House. I was eating a jam sandwich when I remembered
I forgot something in my car. So I went outside to my car
to get my swimming trunks I left in the glove compart-

---

*The Cumberland County Religious Regional Theater is now THE
BOOBY TRAP DISCO. A transvestite bar.

ment. I had left them in there after a midnight swim at a La Quinta Motel. When I opened the car door to retrieve my swimsuit a squirrel distracted me. I accidentally closed the car door on my finger. Well, I let out a stream of obscenities you wouldn't believe. S*it! As*ho*e! Qu**r! Oh boy, that hurt. F*g! Oh yeah! Woo hoo! That was something.

Then there was the time I remember when the boys from the White House Press Corp came down to Missouri to sit a spell and talk politics. I had remembered I had to go to my car to get a pair of Flip Flops that I left in there. 'Come on with me boys,' I said. 'I got to get my Flip Flops.' Well, wouldn't you know it. I did it again. That same squirrel distracted me. As I was retrieving my Flip Flops from the back seat I accidentally slammed my car door on my finger. Oh yeah, that hurt. Fu*k!! Co*k s*ck! Gay Co*k! Bad. Oh boy. Qu**r!! That was a rough one.

Now I like to take credit for a lot of things. Who doesn't? Huh? One year a fella came to me and said that he owned the local donut shop in town. He said he was experimenting with selling the middle of the donut that he took out. And he was calling it a donut hole for now but out of deep esteem and respect for me as the President Of The United States he wanted to call it the "Harry S. Hole". I declined. I said just keep callin' it the donut hole. I hope I don't slam my hand in the car door again. Co*k suc*kin', moth**fuc*in' piece of sh*t!! The fu*k stops here!" (Big applause)

Kelsey Pinto eventually landed a job as Ambassador to Belgium where he insulted a Dignitary's wife and he ended up running a laundry in Spain. He did a very nice job with shirts. I have not heard of him to date.

We need to find a cure for this disease! I have given money.

Vermont Life

MAGAZINE

December 23, 2002

Ed Broth
10153 1/2 Riverside Dr.
#241
Toluca Lake, CA 91602

Dear Ed Broth:

Thank you very much for your query. Unfortunately, it does not suit our current publishing needs. As you are aware, *Vermont Life*'s mission is a broad one; to sketch a general portrait of the state, its people, its history and its achievements.

Accomplishing all of this within the limits of a quarterly challenges us to pick carefully among the many ideas that are submitted and to spread our editorial focus broadly over the state.

Thank you for thinking of *Vermont Life*.

Very truly yours,

Editor

Ed Broth
10153 ½ Riverside Dr.
#241
Toluca Lake, CA 91602

Mr. Editor
VERMONT LIFE MAGAZINE

Jan 16, 2003

Dear Editor,

Thank you for reading my story "TOURETTES SIGN LANGUAGE." I
probably forgot to mention the Vermont references that I have now
sprinkled throughout the story. Sorry!

I am re-sending my story to you. Forgive me, I forgot to really
focus on the Vermont angle here. It is in the story! I hope this
sketches a general portrait of your state, it's people, it's history,
and it's achievements.

Let's get me in your magazine!

With Respect,

Ed Broth

Ed Broth

TOURETTES SIGN LANGUAGE (WITH LOADS OF VERMONT)

My neighbor Kelsey Pinto was recently diagnosed with
TOURETTES SIGN LANGUAGE. This is a disease for people who have Tourettes Syndrome but cannot speak.
Instead they make involuntary obscene gestures at people. They shoot someone the finger, give them the bird,
brush the hand under the chin, grab their crotch with a
"Here's your obscene sign right here, Pal" movement,
bend over and spread their buttocks at you. Things like
that. Now as we all know, Tourettes Syndrome is the disease where one can't help barking out obscenities. These
people can't bark out anything because they can't talk;
but they still have the disease so they have to make
obscene signs at people to let them know they're cursing.

Kelsey Pinto had this disease. He was a mute. **He once
chunked off a big piece of Vermont Cheddar and liked it
very much! It was good cheddar! Like Vermont makes!**
Kelsey would stand on his porch and make involuntary
obscene signs to passerbys. Many a times Mamma
caught a few of his rude "remarks." He would always get
very apologetic and blush then try and have a normal
sign language conversation with Mamma ultimately ending up making more obscene signs: Like the "jerk off"
sign with the hand going up and down or the two fingers
making a hole with another finger going through the
hole. Then he would say he's sorry through sign language: He would shrug his shoulders with a sad face as if
to say, "I can't help myself I have Tourettes Sign Language disease. Bear with me."

That was Kelsey Pinto. He was the fourth grade
teacher at Cumberland Elementary School. They gave

him an educational award once and changed the name of the school to the KELSEY GRAMMAR SCHOOL. (The name Pinto was already used with the College). He showed me his rash once **and told me that Vermont bee-keepers produce several hundred thousand pounds of honey each year. I did not know that.**

Now I had never seen or heard this kind of language before. The closest I came to any filth like this is when a one man show came to town: "HAL HOLBROOK AS HARRY TRUMAN SLAMMING THE CAR DOOR ON HIS FINGER".

Hal Holbrook played Harry Truman—our God fearing, Christian worshiping, highly moral President of the United States who closed the car door on his finger resulting in his letting out a stream of obscenities. Here are a few lines from the play I remember when my parents took me to see it at the Cumberland County Religious Regional Theater one Christmas.* (SEE FOOTNOTE)

FROM THE PLAY:

"Now being President is a pretty darn good thing. I remember one particular day while I was in the White House. I was eating a jam sandwich when I remembered I forgot something in my car. So I went outside to my car to get my swimming trunks I left in the glove compartment. I had left them in there after a midnight swim at a La Quinta Motel. When I opened the car door to retrieve my swimsuit a squirrel distracted me. I accidentally closed the car door on my finger. Well, I let out a stream of obscenities you wouldn't believe. S*it! As*ho*e! Qu**r! Oh boy, that hurt. F*g! Oh yeah! Woo hoo! That was something.

Then there was the time I remember when the boys

---

*The Cumberland County Religious Regional Theater is now THE BOOBY TRAP DISCO. A transvestite bar.

from the White House Press Corp came down to Missouri to sit a spell and talk politics. I had remembered I had to go to my car to get a pair of Flip Flops that I left in there. 'Come on with me boys,' I said. 'I got to get my Flip Flops.' Well, wouldn't you know it. I did it again. That same squirrel distracted me. As I was retrieving my Flip Flops from the back seat I accidentally slammed my car door on my finger. Oh yeah, that hurt. Fu*k!! Co*k s*ck! Gay Co*k! Bad. Oh boy. Qu**r!! That was a rough one.

Now I like to take credit for a lot of things. Who doesn't? Huh? One year a fella came to me and said that he owned the local donut shop in town. He said he was experimenting with selling the middle of the donut that he took out. And he was calling it a donut hole for now but out of deep esteem and respect for me as the President of The United States he wanted to call it the "Harry S. Hole". I declined. I said just keep callin' it the donut hole. I hope I don't slam my hand in the car door again. Co*k suc*kin', moth**fuc*in' piece of sh*t!! The fu*k stops here!" (Big applause)

Kelsey Pinto eventually landed a job as Ambassador to Belgium where he insulted a Dignitary's wife and he ended up running a laundry in Spain. He did a very nice job with shirts. I have not heard of him to date.

Here is another speech from the play "HAL HOL-BROOK AS HARRY TRUMAN SLAMMING THE CAR DOOR ON HIS FINGER" which I remember vividly as a boy. This is where he really gets into the Vermont angle:

"I used to sit on my porch in Vermont—Montpelier—a great American city. (I bought some sneakers there once) Well, one day I was rockin' on my porch when I remembered that I left something in my car. It was the Nagasaki Atom Bomb. I left it there in the hot sun. In my hot car. Sh*t! Pri*k! Fuc*k, what am I a moron? I yelled as I got up from the porch. It must be a 100 degrees in that

hot car. That bomb will go off. And me in the middle of rockin' and eatin' my flapjacks. G*d damn co*k suc*in' gooey Maple Syrup! From Vermont! It used to get cold in Montpelier but not as cold as Burlington, Vermont. (Not affiliated with the Burlington Coat Factory.) Da#mn stinking Maple Syrup got all over me as I rocked and ate those flapjacks. Fu^ck*n' gooey stuff. Tw*t f*rt que*r. I better get that bomb. Qu**r! How I remember the good times in Burlington. The cheddar stops here! I love Vermont! I hope I don't slam my finger in that fu*k*n' car door again because of that nitwit squirrel.

We need to find a cure for this disease! I have given money.

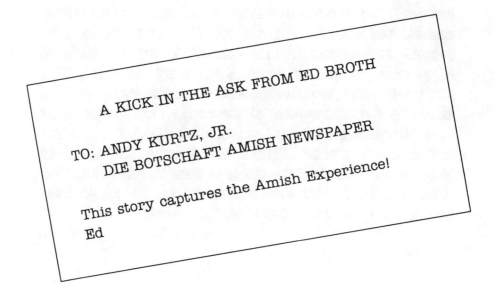

A KICK IN THE ASK FROM ED BROTH

TO: ANDY KURTZ, JR.
DIE BOTSCHAFT AMISH NEWSPAPER

This story captures the Amish Experience!

Ed

MY SCARECROW

I recently put up a scarecrow in my backyard. Recently being a month ago, July. I have been having trouble with gnats. They pester my pumpkin patch. And anything that pesters my pumpkin patch is bad. I grow pumpkins for show. To date I have shown many pumpkins. My scarecrow faces my new neighbor's living room. It is only about 10 feet away from where my new neighbor and his family sit and watch TV and discuss their dreams and hopes as a family.

My scarecrow looks just like my neighbor. It is that bastard Frank Tint. (A disgusting man; a stinko.) My scarecrow has a tuft of blond hair, gray at the sides, a pencil thin moustache (like my neighbor) and the scarecrow's face is ruddy with 2 pockmarks under the nose. Which coincidentally my neighbor (that pri*k Frank Tint) also has near his pencil thin moustache. It is the same height as my neighbor. The straw weighs a few pounds of my neighbor's weight.

I even put my new neighbor's blue denim shirt and tan pants on this scarecrow that my neighbor gave me last winter when he said he was going to throw them away because he couldn't stand them anymore and did I want them? I said I did. (I knew then what I wanted his clothes for.)

The scarecrow scares bugs away. My pumpkins are in bad shape. I have not been able to show anybody these pumpkins in a while. What's the sense of having pumpkins you can't show? Huh? The scarecrow has my neighbor's face, so maybe the gnats are afraid of either my scarecrow or my neighbor's face. But who am I to insult either one?

Once I saw his wife looking at my scarecrow for a long time. Then their curtains closed. Yesterday my ingrate of a neighbor came to me and said he and his family were having trouble watching TV and relaxing with this image of him only 10 feet away. They said that they can't discuss his future, his dreams, what their plans are, their hopes and desires, their successes, their goals, with this scarecrow that looks like him standing there staring in his window. It bothers him he said.

I said "Well, I am sorry, but that was my scarecrow. It was not him. It was just straw and maybe the clothes that he discarded. (And his hat). It's just a scarecrow that guards my pumpkins. It is not you or do I even see the resemblance of you. It is simply a scarecrow that I use to scare away gnats. For my pumpkins."

He said it was him and that I should get rid of it. "Toss it," he said. "Do away with it."

I tasted a macaroon I had eaten a week ago and then said, "Wait a minute, are you saying that my scarecrow is you, and you look as bad as a scarecrow and that you have so little confidence in yourself and your looks that you think you look like a stuffed pile of straw? That's an insult to your wife and the man she married. Plus your family!" I said. "Plus my scarecrow! And my pumpkins. It's all insulting!" I was chagrined. I told him that I guess my scarecrow did the job and scared him. Hah! Too bad he wasn't a gnat. They didn't seem to be coming around anymore and what's important: the gnats not buzzing around my stinky bad pumpkins or my dumb neighbor's idiotic insecurity that he looks like a scarecrow? I smelled pasta salad on his breath. I think it was pasta salad. It could have been something else but I am usually pretty good at identifying lunch smells on people's breath. That's what they must have been eating when he rushed out to anger me again. (We had argued about this pasta smell before.)

Well, the other day my neighbor came running out of his house wearing a too small glittery disco shirt and stretched out clam hopper capri pants. He said that is all he had left after giving most of his clothes away. He said that he had been looking at my scarecrow and he knew that the clothes the scarecrow was wearing were the clothes that he had given me that he was going to throw away. My neighbor approached my scarecrow and said he wanted his clothes back, that they still look pretty good, and that he was asking me nicely for his shirt and pants and hat and scarf back.

I said "Are you telling me that your clothes look better on a straw dummy then they do on you? Is that what you're telling me? Because if it is, then you should stop shopping at the place you're buying your clothes at and wait for someone to give you their old outfits. Because that is what I did. (If you want to look good)."

He said I was ruining his life, the scarecrow was the Devil, and I was bad. I said, "Nonsense. This scarecrow is

NOT the Devil. It is simply a scarecrow. That's all it is. And furthermore, it was protecting my pumpkin patch!"

He stormed back in his house. The sky turned gray. I had not seen a sky this gray since I had rented an M. Night Shyamalan movie at Blockbuster on "Happy Wednesdays." Then I threw a peach pit at his window. To date I have had no more trouble with my neighbor or gnats. But that's to date.

Aug 17, 1999

Dear sir;

Your letter in reference to a scarecrow was received yesterday.

When "Die Botschaft" was started it was decided by a committee to appoint 5 men as a committee to have inspection as to what is printed in Die Botschaft. These 5 appointed men live in 4 different states.

To further clarify, this means we can control what is printed & by whom—, but not who buys the paper.

If The Good Lord lets us live, plans are to have a meeting Sept 7. I will present your letter, but if you prefer I will sent it back to you.

Chairman of Die Botschaft Committee; Andy Kurtz Jr.

Dear Friend Ed.

Andy Kurtz Jr. has passed on close to 2 year ago. and his wife has send me this material. Die Botschaff Committee has rejected this to be printed in Die Botschaff. You might be able to put it in (Plain Interest) magazine of Plain Interest

Die Botschaff Committee

NEW LAWN MOWER

I had just bought the new lawn mower when little Jimmy came over. The receipt said January 23, 2003. I noticed the receipt because I had made an entry into my ATM account to pay for my new lawn mower. "Hey, Mr. Broth, is that your new lawn mower?" Little Jimmy asked me. "Yes, it is, little Jimmy," I said.

"Wow, can I try it?" he said. Naturally, I had to lecture the youth on lawn mower safety before I would even consider letting Jimmy use this machine of a thousand blades. But first I wanted to cut my own grass. I started up the engine and my new mower came to life. Vroom, vroom, I was cutting my grass. And I was telling Jimmy the proper way to mow a lawn. Then it happened. I accidentally ran over my own toe. It popped off like the end of a cigar and Jimmy ran after it. "Is this your toe, Mr. Broth? I think you mowed it off." I told him it was and that we should pack it in ice and then I would go to the hospital and reattach it. (I had already reattached my finger so I knew the game). Plus, I was showing Jimmy the proper way way to carry your own unattached toe in some ice to a hospital.

With my severed toe in a glass of party ice, I showed Little Jimmy how to properly cut the grass. Back and forth we mowed. I told Jimmy that the proper way to cut grass was up and down in a straight line, not zig zagging across the lawn. Vroom, vroom the mower was really moving now. Then it happened. The lawn mover ran over Little Jimmy's toe. His toe popped off like the end of a candy cane. He calmly found the toe in some grass (stuck to a piece of old Seezes candy—caramel center) and we both drove to the hospital in my Plymouth Primavera. This is Plymouth's sassy new sportabout hatchflatch mini bus-car. I like it! (I only have 2,000 more pay-ments).

At the hospital the doctors commended us both for finding the toes, preserving them in ice, and acting sensibly and quickly. They gave us both certificates. We had our operations and we went home.

The next day I took off my shoe and noticed it. I had Jimmy's toe attached to my foot. I was sure it was his toe as my toe had a freckle on it and this toe did not. (Plus I am a 57 year old man with small feet and Jimmy is 13 and Black. I called him up and told him I thought I had his toe and maybe he had mine by mistake. He said he would take a look when he took his sock off but right now he was going to practice field goals in the vacant field.

Later on he called and confirmed that he did indeed have my toe on his foot. Neither of us said anything else about it that summer and we both now go on living with each other's toes.

September 5, 2003

Ed Broth
10153 ½ Riverside Drive #241
Toluca Lake, CA 91602

Dear Mr. Broth:

The biennial Harry S. Truman Book Award competition was established in 1963 for recognition of the best book written within a two-year period dealing primarily and substantially with some aspect of the history of the United States between April 12, 1945 and January 20, 1953, or with the public career of Harry S. Truman. The award is intended to recognize a book-length manuscript.

The Institute very much appreciates your interest in our competition; however, I must return your short story because it does not meet the requirements. We wish you the best in all your future endeavors.

Sincerely,

Office Manager

HARRY S. TRUMAN LIBRARY INSTITUTE

ED BROTH
10153 ½ Riverside Dr.
#241
Toluca Lake, CA 91602

Office Manager
Harry S. Truman Library Institute
Harry S. Truman Library

Oct 3, 2003

Dear Office Manager,

Thank you very much for reading my story and explaining to me the Harry S. Truman Book Award requirements.

Perhaps I forgot to send you the rest of the manuscript. It is not a short story but a novel and the correct title is: "New Lawn Mower The Complete Novel Involving The Harry S. Truman Presidency"

It is a 645 page novelette that deals with a lawn mower, a toe, and Mr. Truman's Presidency. I have enclosed the first page so you can get an idea of the breadth and scope of this work.

I am sorry if I didn't send you the correct story. You may have received a different story in error.

I appreciate it if you would consider this new lawn mower story as it deals with Harry S. Truman, President of the United States from 1945 to 1953, for inclusion in your book award contest.

Thank you for your consideration.

Respectfully,

Ed Broth

Ed Broth

NEW LAWN MOWER:
THE COMPLETE NOVEL
INVOLVING THE
BREADTH & SCOPE OF THE
HARRY S. TRUMAN PRESIDENCY

Chapter 1.

Now let me just tell you Jimmy and I came back from the hospital with our toes attached and who should be standing there? Harry S. Truman himself, that's who. The President of the United States. (This was in 1953. January 19th. The entire book, 645 pages, takes place on that day, on that lawn, and with that mower.)

While my toe was bandaged, President Truman's hand was bandaged. Apparently he slammed it into his car door by mistake. "That pesty squirrel," said President Truman. "I was just getting some swim trunks out of my car, a 1953 Pontiac Pesto, and this squirrel distracted me and wouldn't you know it the car door slammed on my finger." He muffled some foul words. But I distinctly heard "sh*t ba#t*rd co*k s^ck$n fag@ot Fedgermann." You would have thought that Mr. Truman on the next to last day of his Presidency would have spent it elsewhere then on a lawn with 2 fellas who had just mowed a lawn. But he didn't. That's the kind of homesy fella Harry S. Truman was. "Let me show you fellas how to mow a lawn," he said, and he took hold of that big mower, the machine of a thousand blades, and had at it. Vroom, vroom, vroom went that huge mowing machine and Harry Truman zig zagged around the yard mowing up a storm. "THAT'S HOW YOU DO IT!!" he screamed above the mower noise. THIS IS

HOW YOU MOW A LAWN!!!" Jimmy and I watched from a safe distance with our toes bandaged.

Then it happened. Harry S. Truman accidentally ran over his own toe. His toe popped off. Just flew off like a seed from a watermelon. (It landed in the wet grass stuck to a piece of Seezes candy. Nougatty pecan center.) "SH*T, AS#HO#E QU^*R!! he yelled. I NEED THAT TOE!!! THE LUCK STOPS Here!!!

Jimmy and I scooped up the presidential toe from the wet grass, unstuck the old candy, and put the toe on a snow cone that Little Jimmy was eating. (To keep the toe on ice. We learned this from before.) At the hospital the doctors commended us for finding the toe, acting sensibly, and not ruining the snow cone. It was strawberry. It could have been blackberry but then again it could have been strawberry. I am usually good at identifying snow cone flavors but this one had me bewilderd.

Harry S. Truman left office the next day with 9 toes. He never had that toe reattached. He simply led his life like the great man he was; admired and worshipped by many, held in the highest esteem, acclaimed and with a library. (And 9 toes) The pecan nougatty Seezes candy now sits in the Cumberland County Presidential Museum.

644 more pages to come.

THE SMOG CERTIFICATE

I needed to get a smog certificate to get my car regis-
tered. It is a state law in California, this being 2003. For
the record I drive a Ford Pasta Fazool. This is Ford's
rugged European answer to the Hyundai Grouper. (The
minivan that can carry a large contingent of people).

Back to my smog certificate story: The smog certificate is on the state flag. The flag has a bear on it with a
fish in its mouth and smog coming from a car exhaust.
The whole state flag is too crowded and I have told them
so. To date I have not heard a reply. They must be busy
over there. I am sure I am not the only driver. To
describe myself: I am a portly man, almost 5 feet tall
with a 59 inch waist, boils. I treat these boils with
Desenex and have them under control. I wear a size XXL
shirt which I believe at one time was an old football
league. I do have a weight problem and have had one for
some time. My doctor said that his goal for me this year
is to get me back to being heavy. "If we can get you back
to the weight you had your heart attack at, then we are
making progress. You have a lot of work to do to just get
back to being out of shape." I agreed. In consultation
with my dentist, my dentist told me my teeth were
exhausted. I told him to put my x-rays in a pita wrap and
schedule me for a March 2009 cleaning. He contained a
noise.

To continue my story: I pulled into a gas station that
advertised smog certificates. One of the smog workers
motioned me to drive my car closer to him. He kept
motioning me to inch closer. I was inching closer and
closer and finally I drove over his foot. I heard a crunching sound. And I saw him make a face I only saw once
before in "The Exorcist". He was dirty looking and I

could tell he had B.O. I did not know what this B.O. was. It was coming from a jelly stain on his shirt. It could have been raspberry jelly, but then again it could have been boysenberry. I didn't know. I was usually pretty good with recognizing and identifying various jelly stains but this one had me stumped.

Together we maneuvered the car onto the lift. I told him my car drives like a clock. I said "I wish it would drive like a car." I made a joke; he did not laugh. He chattered his teeth like a man sitting in snow. I said "Have you ever been frozen in ice by a man named Roberto?" He said "NO!" He hooked my car up to a machine. He told me the machine was the state smog machine and that it would give him a reading. I saw his name tag, it said Amir. He told me he was from Bazznazio. I contained a belch. My eyes watered. His teeth chattered. We must have been some sight. I asked him "Where can I change into paper underpants? They're medicated, I announced."

He said he didn't know. But I knew he did. I asked him again: "Have you ever been frozen in ice by a man named Roberto? So frozen you drip on carpeting?" He said "No!. This time with more conviction. But I felt he was just giving me smog talk. I have heard this kind of talk before in my circle of friends.

There was no time for idle talk with this foreigner who smelled liked boysenberry. We had work to do. He told me his dream: He wanted to open up a "JFKFC CHICKEN RESTAURANT" where the workers talked like John F. Kennedy and wore funny paper hats and sold chicken. He thought it was a good idea. We both looked under the hood. He said "Here, see this? This is where I am going to hook the machine up to. Then we will get a reading and see what is needed. This reading has to be a 75. It is now 60. I must get it up to 75 to give you a pass." I said "Will you defog me?" Under the hood he said, "Look closer." I put my head more into the car. Then Amir said, "I must kiss you. I find you so attractive that I must put my mouth on yours and kiss you." He tried to put his arm around me and pull me closer. I struggled with him. (I am a heavy person.)

I said, "Please, Mister, I'm just here to get my smog certificate. I don't want to be kissed." I pushed him away. He said, "I must have you. Kiss me back. Take me. I am full of desire for you. I am burning. I am on fire. Take me in your arms." I said, "Get away from me. I feel nothing for you. Is my car almost finished?" He said yes and continued working. I said "Tug my flap." Then he made a face that I have only seen before in "Halloween 9". The whites of his eyes showed and three 7's came across his pupils. He made a noise like a slot machine and nickels shot out of his ear. He leaned back and yelled I JUST PAID OFF!! Then he collapsed. He went down in five stages like an Ikea dining room table with two leaves. I poured tuna water on him and he got up in three stages like a groggy Rhino on the Veterinarian Channel.

Amir finished the job and gave me my smog certificate. I paid him his money ($51.07 worth of burnt almond candy) and drove off. I made a mental note to dislike this man in the future. I may have some more of this story later.

8484 Wilshire Blvd., Suite 900 • Beverly Hills, CA 90211 • 213-651-5400 • FAX 213-651-2741

Thanks for your recent submission to HUSTLER magazine. Unfortunately, we are not able to use this piece at this time. Feel free to send written queries to our offices for future feature considerations. Again, thanks for your interest in HUSTLER.

Sincerely,

HUSTLER Editorial

Stories of
Faith
and
*Determination**
***Plus Cartoons*

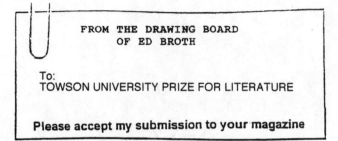

THE FURTHER ADVENTURES OF THE FUNNY CARTOON
"UH, OH, I JUST CUT OFF MY TOE."   BY Ed Broth

"Uh, oh, I just cut off my toe."

January 16, 2003

Ed Broth
10153-1/2 Riverside Dr., #241
Toluca Lake, CA 91602

College of Liberal Arts

Towson University

Dear Mr. Broth:

Thank you for your inquiry about the Towson University Prize for Literature. Unfortunately, the deadline has passed for the 2002 competition; however, I will place your name on the mailing list to receive the 2003 nomination form. This will be sent to you in late spring.   In the meantime I am enclosing a 2002 nomination form which describes the rules of the prize and which may be helpful to you.

Again, thank you for your interest in the Towson University Prize for Literature and please contact our office if you have any questions.

Sincerely,

Administrative Assistant

Enclosure

MY BOYHOOD

I grew up in the heart of Cumberland County. The town was named after Robert County, the founder of Cumberland County. Cumberland County is a novelty gag town with bitter cold winters and dry, waterless hot summers. In the winter it can get down to 22 below zero and you need an extra pair of socks but in the summer it can get as hot as 112 degrees and you can cook eggs in a pan on the stove in the kitchen. It was so hot one summer I once saw a cockroach wearing a canteen. It was just moving across the kitchen floor with a little thing of water slung across its back. Every few steps it would take a sip.

Since this was a company town, most of the people in the community worked for one of the many NOVELTY GAG COMPANIES that had factories all through Cumberland County. Most everybody in town made some type of novelty gag product: phony vomit, fake dog doo, gag snot, artificial medical dribble, chattering teeth, etc. It was estimated that 92 per cent of the county worked for a gag manufacturing company. The other 8 percent were waiters.

There were 29 of those gag companies and factories were humming day and night to meet the demand. Like any factory town it kept the people working and nearly everyone was always coming up with a new novelty. Talk in the diners was always, "Hey, Rick, what do you think of this phony hair on soap and bring me another cup of coffee please." Or "Hey, Margaret, honey, can I get a tuna sandwich today and what about this rubber pencil? Do you think that's funny? And give me a side of cole slaw with that sandwich." Some of the community talked about global warming, weapons of mass destruction, Condoleezza Rice, Korean nuclear weapons, and the demolition of the earth through toxic poison gas but mostly everyone talked about some new gag: a fake banana peel, a hand buzzer, a fly in the ice cube or whatnot. And I wonder to this day if the waiters and waitresses got tired of everyone always asking their opinions about some sort of silly prank toy. Later on when they opened up the Cumberland County Insane Asylum I posed this question to many patients but all I got was real dribble.

My best boyhood friend in Cumberland County was Danny. His dad was a foreman at the CUMBERLAND COUNTY GAG WORKS which was built in 1898 and was the oldest novelty gag company in the county. His dad was a Quality Control Inspector. It was his job to check on the rubber vomit and make sure all the fake ingredients were in there in equal parts. Once in awhile too many green peppers got on there and not enough meatball and the phony vomit had to be thrown away. His dad was honored many times by the community for exemplary service and had many plaques in his home which had the words "phony" and "fake" and "bogus" and "false" and "mock" on the plaques. Danny was proud of his dad. And his dad always had new gag prototypes around the house: Fake oil spill, fictitious glass eye, mock crab meat (which some said would never sell but eventually was bought by the Lee Kemp company and shipped worldwide and eaten by everyone! It was dee-licious!)

Danny and I did everything together. Danny made a homemade pipe bomb one summer from oily rags he found in his dad's hamper and accidentally blew off his hand. Then in the winter, Danny found some dynamite in his dad's sock drawer and accidentally blew off his foot. Lucky it was on the other side of his blown off hand so Danny could still lean. Then 2 summers later Danny was working with pharmaceutical nitrate, phosphate, fly paper, and old baloney which he found in his dad's underwear drawer, and accidentally lost an eye. I went by Danny's house and stole out of his dad's hamper because he could not see me from that side. (I still have his son's socks. But, hey, with one foot what does he care?) Huh?

Then a few years later when we were both 16 Danny was fooling around with some sparklers he found in the back of his dad's prosthetic cabinet and accidentally blew off the top of his head. They sewed it back on at the hospital using old newspapers, straw, and the top of a basketball. He did NOT look funny but his dog refused to sniff him anymore. A few years after that Danny found some firecrackers and blew off his neck. His head sat on his shoulders for some time. (I bought him a hat; his dad reprimanded him for bringing firecrackers into the home.)

Danny is now a Supreme Court Judge. All that's left of him is a thumb and part of his lap. Good thing he gets to wear a robe. He makes very important decisions. I tire of this story. I am leaving for now.

Sandlapper
Society, Inc.

Lexington, South Carolina 29071

February 23, 2004

Mr. Ed Broth
101531½ Riverside Drive, #241
Toluca Lake, CA 91602

Dear Mr. Broth:

Thanks for sending "My Boyhood." Because *Sandlapper* publishes only articles that pertain to South Carolina, we'll have to decline your submission.

Enclosed are our guidelines, which will give you more information about our editorial operation.

Best wishes for your writing.

Sincerely,

managing editor

Sandlapper Society, Inc. is a 501(c)(3) non-profit educational organization dedicated to promoting the positive aspects of our state through
Sandlapper,® *The Magazine of South Carolina*

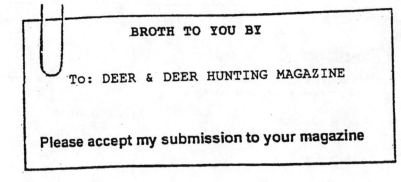

RICARDO THE PIECE OF FUDGE   BY ED BROTH

"Do these shoes make me look taller?"

DEER &
DEER HUNTING
MAGAZINE

January 23, 2003

Ed Broth
10153 ½ Riverside Drive # 241
Toluca Lake, CA 91602

Dear Mr. Broth,

Thank you for submitting your cartoon for my review and consideration.

Although I found the cartoon interesting, it does meet my upcoming editorial needs. More specifically, we do not publish cartoons at this time in the magazine. Still, thanks for your interest in *Deer & Deer Hunting* magazine.

Sincerely,

Managing Editor

RUDY THE CONTORTIONIST

One summer growing up in Cumberland County Daddy's brother came to visit us. His name was Rudy. Rudy Broth. And he made his living as a rubber man in a carnival. He was a contortionist; he could bend his body in many ways. He was the rubber brother. That's what everyone referred to him as in the family. His stage name was Rudy Delapeep. He thought Delapeep was more glamourous then Broth. And I have to admit he was right. I tried at one time to get Daddy to call himself Daddy Delapeep because Rudy was so glamorous with his glittery show business job and all but Daddy refused. "I got my own problems," Daddy would say. "I got a rash."

Sometimes Rudy would sit with his leg over his head and drink coffee that way. It was disgusting but what could I do? I would say to Daddy, "Uncle Rudy has his left leg up and around over his neck and is holding the coffee cup with his toe. I can see stuff*." Daddy would say "What do you want me to do? Say something to Rudy? Older men at the beach show the same thing. Live with it. He's a contortionist. He's in a glamorous glittery profession. Look at his spangly costume." I said "Yes, but the older men at the beach have netting there in their swimsuits and are NOT contortionists." My Daddy just shrugged and sat there with his blintz and apple juice as Rudy just sipped his coffee with his leg over his neck and his chuckles* flapping in the wind like he didn't have a care in the world. Rudy didn't care about us. It was disgusting. Daddy would say, "He's in show business, your Uncle Rudy. He's glamourous and glittery. He's in the same business as Frank Sinatra and Jumpy The Horse.

One time a neighbor said to us "Your Daddy's brother had his leg up over his head at the supermarket. We saw

him at the deli counter and he was balancing on his right hand with both legs up so it looked like he was talking through his butt. His butt was definitely sticking out there in the deli lady's face. I could hardly keep my mind on my potato salad."

I said "He was Rudy The Contortionist. He was a rubber man in a carnival. You may have known him as

Rudy Delapeep. He bent himself up like this." They would say "We can see the rim of his underwear." I said "I bet you could if he was talking through his butt." But they didn't care that he worked for the carnival. To the people in the supermarket it was just a disgusting man flapping his chimichongas* at the counter help. "He's no Sinatra," they would say. And you know something—deep down inside they were right.

CHIMICHONGAS

The carnival closed that winter and Daddy's brother, Rudy, came to live with us permanently. He stayed in the laundry room with the bleach.

Another time Rudy was waiting in line at the local movie theater (A Cary Grant movie was playing; I think it was "The Man With The X-ray Vest". That was it. No wonder it didn't do well. Like the Man With the X-ray Eyes. Or "The Man With The X-ray Visions." This was just a vest and if you had an X-ray you wore the vest. So what's the big deal? Anyway, I happened to be coming out of a "Furrell's Good Time Ice Cream Parlor" with Teenie when we saw Rudy. He was third in line and he had both legs behind his neck balancing on his hand. You could see his potato chips* just flapping away there while he balanced. It was disgusting! And Teenie looked away. But I could see and I whispered in Rudy's ear: "Your coconut heads* are exposed. Please cover them up. This is the line for a Cary Grant movie. There are females here. Women." And I looked at Teenie. She was eating her ice cream; that's all she cared about.

Rudy simply said, "I am a contortionist. I am a rubber man. I bend myself up. I twist myself around. I am in a glamorous, glittery profession. The people come and see me like they line up for Cary Grant. I can't help what

you think, you and your dirty thoughts. What's what is what's what. People want to see thrills when they see a contortionist. I give it to them."

Then there was the time when Daddy got Rudy a job as a pretzel maker, working the counter at the local pretzel store. He had his legs completely wrapped around the top of his head and he was wearing a bathing suit. This was the most disgusting. Standing there with a pretzel store full of people and his headlights* were almost completely exposed to the people buying pretzels.

I stood in line and when I reached Rudy I said, "I know you're family, but do you have to stand there with your bean bags* out there in the pretzel line?

He said "Look at the pretzel. Am I any different? I'm a contortionist, a rubber man, I'm just giving the people a sensation. Like the pretzel. It's twisted. They like that."

And I must admit he had a point. Who am I to judge?

---

*kumquats.

Arthritis Today

Dear Freelancer:

Thank you for submitting your idea to Arthritis Today. Unfortunately, the idea that you describe does not fit our needs at this time.

Please feel free to submit other articles or ideas that you feel might be appropriate for our readership. Again, thank you for thinking of Arthritis Today.

Sincerely,

Assistant Editor

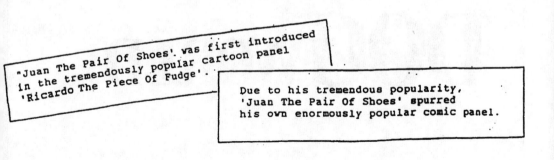

"Juan The Pair Of Shoes' was first introduced
in the tremendously popular cartoon panel
'Ricardo The Piece Of Fudge'.

Due to his tremendous popularity,
'Juan The Pair Of Shoes' spurred
his own enormously popular comic panel.

JUAN THE PAIR OF SHOES   By ED BROTH

"Uh, oh, I stepped on some fudge"

DOGWORLD

Ed Broth
10153 1/2 Riverside Dr.
#241
Toluca Lake, CA 91602

Dear Mr. Broth:

**Thank you very much for your letter. Unfortunately, we will
not be able to use your cartoon, "Juan, The Pair Of Shoes,"
because we do not run cartoons in DOG WORLD.**

Sincerely,
The Staff of DOG WORLD

THE FURTHER ADVENTURES OF THE FUNNY CARTOON
"UH, OH, I JUST CUT OFF MY TOE."   BY ED BROTH

"Uh, oh, I just cut off my toe."

THE MAGAZINE OF MONEY-MAKING OPPORTUNITIES

SPARE TIME

Dear colleague:

Thank you for the article you suggested to us. Unfortunately, we won't be able to use it in the forseeable future, so I'm returning your materials to you. I'm also enclosing our Writer's Guidelines and our current Editorial Calendar, to give you an idea of what and how to write for SPARE TIME.

Thank you for your interest. Looking forward to hearing from you again, I am ...

Sincerely yours,

editor

300,000
GUARANTEED
CIRCULATION
PER ISSUE

Increasing Advertisers' Sales
For Over 40 Years!

BIG MANS PANTIES

I had been buying "BIG MANS Panties" for some time now. At least since 1999. These are a mens panty that a big man—6'4" and 290 pounds would wear. Mostly truckers, dockworkers, tree trimmers—anywhere you see a big man chances are they're wearing panties. Go to the mall and watch a really big guy coming out of Sears with a Kenmore chainsaw. Chances are he has on a pair of panties. Ask him. Say to him "Pardon me, sir, are you wearing Big Man's Panties?" He is! Go to a truck dealership and see a very big man looking at a Dodge Durango. When he's finished ask him if he's wearing panties. Chances are he is.

Let me just say here these are NOT ladies underwear! This is simply a panty that a big man likes to wear. Some big men just like a looser fitting undergarment. That's why Big Mans Panties are so popular and are gaining in popularity throughout the Tri Region.

Usually I go to "LEE PLINKOWITZ'S BIG MANS PANTY STORE" in the Crestview Mall to buy my big mans panties. I like the way they treat you at Lee Plinkowitzs and they always have a nice selection. Plus, Lee comes out of the back and will always measure you correctly. (When he hears big men rustling around by the panties he always comes out from the back with his measuring tape) Plus, I like his ads on TV too: "Come on down to Lee Plinkowitz's Big Mans Panty Store in the Crestview Mall. If you're a big man—a trucker or a dock worker—and like to wear a nice sheer nylony panty we have 'em in big man sizes. Starting at double X all the way to size 65 waist. Remember, if you can find a cheaper panty in the mall our panty is Freeeee!"

I like when Lee says "Freeeee" at the end of the commercial. Like he got stuck on a letter and just said it until the air came out. Plus they give you cookies and hot dogs down there if you come in and browse and I like that I can leave my business card and get a chance on a free trip to Cabo San Luco. I once went there and had an itch and ended up on a shrub scratching it.

Sometimes Lee comes out of the back and shakes his toupee at you. Some white sprinkle falls off. Plus, they have 3 new colors!—Bauge, flant, & turtle which is a kind of brownish-greenish color that goes good on mens panties. Yesterday they had SNIFFY THE CLOWN at their new store. "Take a picture in your panties with Sniffy!" they advertised all over the mall. And lots of men lined up to take a picture with Sniffy The Clown.

Later on I saw Sniffy eating at the El Toroto Restaurant in the Mall. He was having a chimichonga and had red sauce and peppers on his shirt that he did not wipe off.

Sniffy is a fixture around town. I have also seen him in the street disoriented after working at "THE THREE HOLE PUNCH SHACK" to mingle with the customers. The Three Hole Punch Shack is a hole punch super store. It is probably the biggest store in Cumberland County and all they sell are three hole punches. These are the tools that you use when you want to put three holes in your paper and then put the paper in a binder. You would be surprised how popular these are and how many different types there are. Last time I was in their Super Store on Flemson—there are 2 of them in Cumberland County— they had to close the store because too many people were in there. One man was eating a sandwich when they removed him. (Low carb Bologna)

I continue my story: Lee once advertised Panties—1/2 off!! I didn't know if the panties were worn half off or they were half off the price. Lee corrected me. He was that kind of guy to his customers. He said, "No the panties are half off the price. Not worn half off."

So it was to my surprise that yesterday I read in the paper that Lee Plinkowitzs Big Mans Pantys in the mall (Crestview) is closing. My mail order Russian wife, Duoc Tieng Mot, was also surprised. In fact she was the one who told me.

She said "Did you know that Lee Plinkowitz's is closing?"

I said I did not and belched up a macaroon. Some coconut spittled onto her. She looked at it, I looked at her, then she looked at me again. To my knowledge that coconut spittle is still there. Althought as this point in time I wonder If I should really buckle down and look.

We found out about the closing when we were in the mall yesterday looking for a book that I had heard about called "The Threat Of Drizzle". This was a book about a big mans adventure in the everyday world and the possibility that it may drizzle that day and he could get wet. He didn't want to get wet so he was afraid of the drizzle.

Waldinn Books said it was sold out but they said they would order it for me if I made a face and turned around slowly for the clerk. I did not. I thought that was strange behavior and told them so. They just smirked and said if you want the book, do it! (I ended up ordering the book on Amazon. It was very good. The man got drenched at the end. I am sorry if I gave away the story.) I am tired now. But that, so far, is some of my story.

Gourmet

THE MAGAZINE OF GOOD LIVING

560 Lexington Avenue · New York, N.Y. 10022

We regret that we cannot use the enclosed material, but appreciate your submitting it to us.

The Editors

The Tampa Herald

/ WEDNESDAY, JANUARY 15, 2003 / **BUSINESS** —

Study traces steps to fiasco

Multiple problems led to energy crisis

by Jennifer Coleman
Associated Press

SACRAMENTO — Califor-
ia's energy crisis cost the state
s muc
ears i
st bu
nd a
owth
e Pr
alifo
The
onclu
ause
hich
000-0
olling
A
enera
market
ttemp
rator

Ne
at
Bi
Vide
Tues
dent
posit
State
In
assun
mark
tional
Unite
was t
by Jin
of W
replac
chief
Oil
due
Th
in V
with
price
Autor
Calif

regulatory missions all con-
Christopher Weare, a research mark
the state regula-

"Electricity sector restr
turing followed by crisis has l
to an ad hoc and confusing m
of state agencies and depa
ments," the report said.

PANTY STORE OWNER ARRESTED

Store was a phony operation say Police

By Lou Snyder
Herald Staff Writer

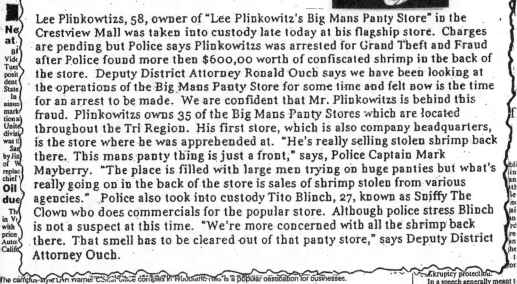

Lee Plinkowtizs, 58, owner of "Lee Plinkowitz's Big Mans Panty Store" in the Crestview Mall was taken into custody late today at his flagship store. Charges are pending but Police says Plinkowitzs was arrested for Grand Theft and Fraud after Police found more then $600,00 worth of confiscated shrimp in the back of the store. Deputy District Attorney Ronald Ouch says we have been looking at the operations of the Big Mans Panty Store for some time and felt now is the time for an arrest to be made. We are confident that Mr. Plinkowitzs is behind this fraud. Plinkowitzs owns 35 of the Big Mans Panty Stores which are located throughout the Tri Region. His first store, which is also company headquarters, is the store where he was apprehended at. "He's really selling stolen shrimp back there. This mans panty thing is just a front," says, Police Captain Mark Mayberry. "The place is filled with large men trying on huge panties but what's really going on in the back of the store is sales of shrimp stolen from various agencies." Police also took into custody Tito Blinch, 27, known as Sniffy The Clown who does commercials for the popular store. Although police stress Blinch is not a suspect at this time. "We're more concerned with all the shrimp back there. That smell has to be cleared out of that panty store," says Deputy District Attorney Ouch.

The campus-style LNR Warner Center office complex in Woodland Hills is a popular destination for businesses.

Valley offices still building

NR / From Page 1

akruptcy protection.
In a speech generally meant t
buoy the morale of the compa
ny's 60,000 employees world
wide, Capellas said WorldCom
the No. 2 long-distance carrie
after AT&T, would continue to
develop new products for con
sumers and business customers

Stories of
Fortitude
and
Purpose

PART 2 OF THE HOTEL HONOR BAR STORY

Well, here I am in the middle of my book. Like I said I am a traveling salesman. A pretty darn good one. I think. I stage Civil War Reenactments with hens. I dress these hens in the Blue & Gray uniforms of the North and South Armies of the Civil War and watch them reenact famous battles. It is something to see these hens relive Gettysburg charging straight ahead with their muskets. I want to just say here that no hens are harmed in any way during these reenactments. I want to be emphatic here. No hen is injured or mistreated. We care for these hens to insure their safety and well being. We simply enjoy the show eating a nice chicken dinner or maybe some eggs. (For those that are sick of chicken.) We will NOT HARM these hens in any way. I am EMPHATIC ABOUT THAT!!

As a salesman I am on the road a lot. I drive a Buick Tortolini. This is Buick's sporty little answer to the Humvee Hummer. (It can go offroad anywhere). And today I find myself in Peppermint, Nevada staying at the WESTINNE CHOY TUAN DING HOTEL. I would have to say that the Westinne Chain is the finest hotel chain out there. They are very courteous to travelers. (Of which I am one) They make sure of your every need, fill all your expectations, and have good comforters. I would recommend the Westinne to anyone. (Who asks) This is a Mobile Gold Leaf, Class A-, 12 Star, Fidgety Hotel. I like the Westinne Choy Tuan Ding because I get to look out my hotel room window at the parking lot. Once I saw a soda delivery man unloading Shasta. He spilled some orange. Another time I saw a lion roaming in the parking lot and actually chew a man in half. No one else saw it and I wished I had my video camera with me so I could sell it to Brazilian TV for one of their "Pets" shows. I have 59 channels of Brazilian TV on my cable system. The manager at this hotel is Tony Yawn. See him for special needs.

BACK TO MY HONOR BAR STORY: I was in my room when I noticed the Honor Bar. Or Mini Bar as many call it. To refresh: The Honor Bar is locked and comes with a key. They have soda and candy and chips in there. You want something you mark it down and pay them later. They are relying on you to tell them what you marked down, what you ate. "This is an honor system we have here, Mr. Broth," the hotel manager said to me as I checked in. "We leave the candy and chips in your room. On an honor basis. If you want them just mark it down and pay us later. We operate honorably." He gave me a full grin I gave him a half smirk. (We were both professionals)

Now let me say here that these hotel people have a keen eye. The hotel people are not run by stupes. If you screw with them they will hunt you down like an animal. They will pursue you like a fugitive. To wit: I tried to take a package of Fritos without paying for it and a dye pack exploded on me. I opened the bag of chips and purple ink got all over my face. Within moments a Security Guard was at my door and I was escorted through the lobby with dye all over my skin. Many people noticed. There were whispers.

That evening I went down to the hotel lounge and noticed that one of my favorite singing groups was performing. The sign outside said:

IN OUR LOUNGE
SH*T, SHOWER, & SHAVE SING THE SONGS OF EARTH,
WIND, & FIRE

These guys are good! This was a tribute band and these fellas looked like Earth, Wind, and Fire. They had their sound down, had the big Afros, and white jumpsuits that were so tight you could see the outline of a stretch mark on Shave. Any time I got to make it to Peppermint, Nevada I always stay at this particular hotel and I always see this group singing there. They must have been there 20 years. Tonight I sat at the bar after their set and conversed with the group.

Now Shower and Shave didn't mind their names but you should have seen the other guy complain. He griped he could never meet anyone. And it still bothered him after 22 years when someone called out: "Hey Sh-t. You gonna sing "Reasons" tonight?" "Yo, __! How about "Shinin' Star"? You gonna sing it?" Once Shower was mistaken in the airport when this gentleman said to him "Are you __? You sure look like Sh*t. I chuckled while the real Sh-t steamed at the other end of the bar. I detected some uneasiness. He said, "You know after 23 years I never get used to it. But I still look back when they call my name."

I put five cough drops in my mouth (Ludens) and listened to their stories as they continued to drink. That night at the bar sure was fun. It gets lonely on the road and these 3 guys were sure good company. I gave them some free samples that I always give out to my customers: Combs and key chains and human flesh cream with Hens in Civil War uniforms on them. They told me about their selves and I told them about me. What I do, where I work. I said, "Lots of guys give you a 100 percent. I break it up. I give you 50 percent in the morning and 50 percent in the afternoon. That's a 100 percent in my book."

ENDO

HEALTHY PREGNANCY
BABYTALK
BABYTALK *Childbirth Guide*
BABYTALK *First-Year Guide*

Dear Writer:

Thank you for your submission to *BabyTalk*! Unfortunately, your article does not meet our editorial needs at this time. As always, though, we appreciate your ideas and welcome your continued interest in *BabyTalk*! We look forward to hearing from you again soon.

All the best,
The Editors

SUMMER FUN!

I found a brochure at work that was thrown away. I work as a seeing eye man for a blind dog. I scooped this brochure out of the bin. Now let me just say here that many valuable things are thrown in the bins at work and if you look through the trash like I do when everyone has left work you can find a treasure or two. That's how I got a perfectly good lunchbox with a picture of Hitler on it.

THE COVER OF THE BROCHURE:
ENJOY THE SUMMER AT "LEON FEDGERMANN'S SQUIRREL FANTASY CAMP." LIVE WITH THE SQUIRRELS!!! ENROLLMENT NOW BEING ACCEPTED!!

I was interested. Summer was fast approaching and I wanted to have some fun! And a squirrel fantasy camp sounded like it would be. Fun, that is. (The Squirrel Fantasy Camp).

THE INSIDE OF THE BROCHURE:
LEON FEDGERMANN'S SQUIRREL FANTASY CAMP! Only room for 2612 men ages 57 and up. (Plus room for 1 man aged 18) Over 250,000 squirrels! Wake up with a squirrel on your head. Live with a squirrel on your bunk. Eat breakfast next to a squirrel. Crack an acorn with a squirrel. Do crafts, make things. Everywhere you look—squirrels. If you like squirrels this is the camp for you. Pet a squirrel, feed a squirrel, make friends with squirrels, they are great companions!

All squirrel droppings will be picked up daily! Squirrel barf kept to a minimum this camp. Last years camp is greatly improved. Squirrel bites reduced by 67 percent. Squirrel disease reduced by 15% Squirrel droppings almost gone. Nurse now on duty! (NOTE: If a squirrel runs off into the woods DON'T FOLLOW IT!! Jewelry can be replaced!)

We are now broken into 2 camps: Those who like squirrels, those who don't. We have had many successful camps in the past. Our hyena camp is now closed! Don't be left out. (NOTE: If a squirrel steals your medicines—do NOT follow it into the woods!)

THE BACK OF THE BROCHURE:
Remember, when you think of a lot of squirrels there's only one place to go: Leon Fedgermann's Squirrel Fantasy Camp—off the I-27 near Flotsam Woods. Remember!!! IF A SQUIRREL RUNS INTO THE WOODS. DO NOT CHASE IT!!! I can't be more emphatic about this. Forget your rings and watches and medicines and girly magazines—it's not worth it.

Naturally the brochure intrigued me. I remembered a squirrel running up our tree after it had taken Mamma's torn bra from our clothesline and I thought that I may enjoy this camp. I once petted a squirrel in high school— many years ago—and had to take a series of painful rabies shots. But that was a while ago and anti-venims were now pretty standard. (I was told the camp had a ninety day supply)

I decided to go to this squirrel camp. I had debated about going here or to male shampoo school for the summer. And I can only tell you that I had the most wonderful time at this squirrel fantasy camp. I know there are 322 different squirrel camps operating in the United States but this one is the best. Yes, squirrels ran off with

some of my possessions but I followed the camp coun-
selors orders and did not chase the squirrels into the
woods. I just let whatever I lost go and got on with my
life and enjoyed the camp even though the camp was
closed a few days earlier this year due to "unforeseen
circumstances" I was later told.

I will be back next year to Leon Fedgermann's Squirrel Fantasy Camp.*

---

*In my next Squirrel Camp story—Part 2—I will tell of a few adven-
tures I had at the camp and I will list some of the things I did not
return home with.

BOMB MAGAZINE

May 24, 2004

Dear Mr. Broth,

Thank you for giving *BOMB* magazine the opportunity to consider your work for publication. Unfortunately, it does not meet our needs at this time.

We wish you the best of luck placing your poems elsewhere, and thank you again for submitting it to us.

Sincerely,

The Editors

THE WASH UP TOWN

Bibb County was the next county over from Cumberland County. They were our neighbors and their city was half the size. Most travelers on the way to Cumberland on Interstate G-17 got to Bibb County first and they usually got out of their cars there to gas up, use the washroom, grab a bite or a snack, adjust their trousers, shake out a dress, and spank their kids. Bibb County's slogan was: "Bibb County: Get out of your car, take a leak, adjust your pants, yell at your kid, empty your ashtray, change a diaper, shuffle your dress, urinate, blow your nose, shake out your crumbs, buy a Pepsi, curse a foreigner. 1000 bathrooms! Bibb County. We're the Wash Up Town." (They got all that on the sign.)

They weren't proud of it but that's just the way it was. They were the Wash Up Town and most folks made their living in the wash up industry, the only industry in Bibb County. They supplied paper towels, cleaned commodes, refilled vending machines, ordered Pepsi, danced around in front of your cars with funny hats on, sold souvenirs, squeegeed your window, ogled your wives. One attendant would service your car. (Actually have sex with your car)

Everyone lived on tips. The whole town walked around with pocketfuls of change. All you heard in the evening was "You got a dollar for four quarters?" And "I'd like a beer. Here's 30 dimes. It's 3 dollars. It may be dimes but it's all there."

For 61 years Bibb County was known as The Wash Up Town. People raised families there, got an education, went into the service, became Moonies. There must be 12 generations of Bibbonians in that town. One person was Robert Cocacola and he ran the family soft drink company—Robert's Cola. They were a small soft drink company in

Bibb and they supplied most of the town's vending machines with soda pop. Mr. Cocacola—as most Bibbonians called him—but to others he was Robert or Bob or Robby or Robt. but never Rob. Go figure. Anyway his soda had a loyal following with their caramel Pepsi like tasting drink. It was popular at "The Truck Stops Here" truck stop right when you enter Bibb County.

Another popular Bibbonian was Howie the hard nosed Homo. He was, I think, the only gay fella in town and everybody called him Howie the hard nosed Homo because he never gave much ground. "No," I said. "And that means No!" That's what Howie would always tell people regarding anything. "When I say no, I mean it. No is no. Don't even think of trying to get me to change my mind. I said no! And I mean it. What part of no don't you understand?" Everybody liked Howie very much even though he was hard nosed.

Well . . . They tried everything to get people to stay in Bibb County and not just wash up. They had meetings and more meetings and yet more meetings. "We need an attraction here like Epcot Center," said Sol Bismol, the Mayor of Bibb County. And then his son Pepto, the Councilman, would say "Like Gator World in Orlando. To get people to stay for more then 10 minutes. We need something. An enticement. People got to do more then just pull in, gas up and wash up. We need something that'll get 'em to stay for awhile."

So . . . They opened "BUFFALO BOILS WILD WEST SHOW." Buffalo Boil sold them a bill of goods. He was an ex cowboy that had too many horse rides and he was saddle sore. Yet he attempted to put on a Wild West show. People didn't care. They just filled up their cars with gas, squeegeed their car windows, got a Pepsi, and washed up. Very few stuck around to see an aging cowboy sit up in his saddle uncomfortably and ride around. It closed.

Then . . . They tried the Bibb County Comedy Club, Chortles. They even booked Carob Top, the health nut comedian. Carob Top did an act about turkey burgers, veggie melts, imitation crab. He ate tofu on stage and had other props. People yawned. "Get him out of here!" they yelled. And they did.

Then there was . . . Dinner theater to get people to stay in Bibb County in the evening. Dusty Barron or Busty Darron was the theater manager and after 12 weeks of secret auditions and practice he finally put on the play: "TEDDY ROOSEVELT COUGHING". This was a lively one man play with Teddy Roosevelt (played by Tee-nie's Stepfather Gene Gassy) telling his famous tales of Rough Riders and being President and living in the White House with hacking and coughing in between the tellings. It did not last. People didn't care. They just filled up their cars, threw away a Kleenex, grabbed a Snickers, shook out a dress, and washed up.

Finally . . . The Chef from "The Chef's Diabetic Foot Restaurant" (which had closed due to illness) came into Bibb County from Cumberland with big plans to open up his new eating establishment: "THE CHEF'S PUFFY RIGHT EYE RESTAURANT". Well that caused a stir. Oakie Midows, a local, commented "He did have a successful restaurant in Cumberland. Maybe he could do the same thing here and get people to at least stay awhile and dine."

Me? I just told the Chef he oughta have that right eye looked at." The last I heard he was trying to open a restaurant called "BLAH BLAH BLAH BLAH BLAHS". "So everybody will talk about us," the Chef reasoned. It never opened. (To my knowledge)

This was life in Bibb County. The Wash Up Town. The next county over.

VEGGIE LIFE
GROWING GREEN, COOKING LEAN, FEELING GOOD

June 20, 2004

Veggie Life Magazine

Dear Ed,

Thank you for your interest in Veggie Life. The story you
submitted a while back was interesting, but we are unable to find a
place for it in Veggie Life. We wish you the best of luck in placing
it elsewhere.

Sincerely,

Editor

BIBB COUNTY MINI MALL

Many townsfolks went over to Bibb County which was the next city over from Cumberland County. Bibb County was smaller but had more to offer. For instance, many folks got their coffee at "JITTERS" which had been open in the Mini Mall for some time. It was the only Mini Mall in Bibb County and they only had the one store in there— Jitters. People came there, drank coffee, read the newspaper, and chatted. Jitters was the place to just sit back, relax, and let the world breeze by. It was easy living.

Well wouldn't you know it. A few weeks later a new place opened next to Jitters in the empty store in the Bibb Mini Mall. They sold muffins and apple concoctions and the place was called "FRITTERS". So now folks could get coffee from Jitters and then get a sweet roll right next door at Fritters. Everyone seemed to like this arrangement. Folks thought it was cute and they didn't have to go far to get their coffee or their apple concoction. The Mini Mall was bustling. But still very relaxing with townsfolks drinking their coffee and eating their muffins. Oh sure, there were many empty stores but the new owner, Darryl Crunch, came by and surveyed the mini mall and said: "I vow to fill this place up with stores for the community, that the community wants, that the community needs, that the peoples must have. This will be a community spot. A place to relax." Then he stared in the sun like a seagull waiting for crumbs to fall. (They never did. People didn't give up their crumbs so easily around here.)

Well, wouldn't you know it but two weeks later a brand new pet wash opened in the Bibb Mini Mall. They washed and groomed pets and sprayed these pets with a nice smelling spray. I think it was raspberry but it could have been strawberry. I am usually pretty good at recognizing pet spray smells but this one stumped me. This new pet place was called "CRITTERS". And the people loved it. Many people brought their pets to be groomed, had a fritter, got some coffee, and chatted. It was very relaxing.

Well, things were going great. There were still a few empty stores left but there was one less empty store when it was rented out to a Comedy Cub called "TITTERS". People were laughing and having fun and driving away with their clean pets and apple fritters and laughs. But then there was a problem: Seems there was another comedy club across town with that same name. The comedy club in Cumberland County was also called Titters. They sued. No problem said the Bibb Mini Mall Comedy Club. They simply changed their name to "KIDDERS." And continued to do business. Kidders was really packing them in. People laughing and having fun. And Jitters was doing business. And Critters was busy. Fritters was selling more concoctions that they could imagine. It was all very relaxing.

However, the parking situation was getting messy. I have to admit that. Cars would pull into the parking spot and see the TERS on the concrete and they would go for the spot only to see a TIT in front of the TERS and a sign that said: PARKING ONLY FOR TITTERS. IF YOU WANT TO PARK FOR CRITTERS OR JITTERS FIND THEIR SPOTS. It was a mess. Cars pulled in and and then pulled right out when they realized the parking spot was for the pet store and they wanted an apple sweet. Or they would patently wait for a car to pull out of a parking spot to get coffee, only to see a dog rear his head in the passenger seat and the car pull out and the spot said PARKING FOR CRITTERS ONLY! DON'T EVEN THINK OF PARKING HERE! IF YOU WANT FRITTERS FIND THEIR PARKING SPOT AND PARK THERE!!

The parking situation really got nasty. Cars pulling in and out all day into the wrong parking spots. People holding washed cats and hot coffee and jelly donuts. And dogs barking and howling at the bakery goodies trying to sniff it out of people's hands. I don't think anyone really got their correct parking spot. (I know I didn't) Yes there was cursing. Yes there was anger. Yes there was apple fritter rage. But people had to park. (I am now sorry for some of the rude things I said to those drinking coffee and eating cake. I am truly sorry. I am sorry you were relaxing and I broke it up for you and you took your coffee and cake and sat in your car and ate it).

The Titters people became enraged again. "You changed your name but you didn't change the name on your parking spots," they bellowed. "No problem," said the Bibb Mini Mall Association. (Headed by Darryl Crunch) And immediately the parking spots were changed to Kidders. But they want out of business and a Stop Smoking place took over their store. and "QUITTERS" was put on their parking spot and the parking anger started again on those spots. "YOU CAN'T PARK HERE!!! THIS IS FOR THE STOP SMOKING PLACE. DON'T EVEN THINK OF IT!! WE MEAN IT! Imagine how irritated those people were.

Some curse words were uttered; some foul language was displayed. A finger was seen. Kelsey Pinto made a gesture with his closed palm and a hotdog.

Then the last empty store in the Bibb Mini Mall was rented. Many folks wondered what Shower and Shave from the Earth, Wind, and Fire Tribute band was doing in the Mall without buying anything. "They sure seemed to be here a lot snooping around," said Jim Flesh, a local. "Wonder if they're gonna open a business?" said Ida Plunge, another local who took her coffee every day at Jitters.

Shower and Shave went downtown to the Courthouse (Department Of Business License Applications) and the clerk, Mary Jo Blot, said "I know your partner's name. I just need to know what kind of business this is going to be. Huh?"

I have no more interest in this story. Phooey.

R·U·G
HOOKING

February 25, 2004

Ed Broth
10153 1/2 Riverside Drive
#241
Toluca Lake, CA 91602

Dear Mr. Broth:

Thank you for the submission of your short story "Bibb County Mini Mall," as a possible article in a future issue of *Rug Hooking* magazine.

After reading the article, I feel it is not appropriate to the subject matter of our publication. I am returning the manuscript and wish you well in being able to place it elsewhere.

Sincerely,

Editor
Rug Hooking magazine

BIG MANS TEDDYS

I had been buying "BIG MANS TEDDYS" for as long as I can remember. At least since 2001. This is a Teddy—a frilly sheer wispy lingerie nighty—that a big man wears as relaxing wear.

Now let me set the record straight. This is NOT a naughty sex related garment. Or an arousal type of attire that a woman wears for a man. This is simply a flimsy Teddy a big man wears for comfort. Walk around a mall. See a big man—a guy 6 foot 4 inches and 270 pounds and over coming out of a Big 5 Sporting Goods store with a boat battery. Chances are he wore a Teddy last night. Go ask him. Go up to him and say. "I know you're a big man. What are you about 270 pounds? Maybe 280? What color is the Teddy you wore last night? (Chances are it's red.) Or ask a big man, a 500 pounder, looking at a Chevy Tundra. Ask him about the Teddy he wears. Go up to him—a stranger—and say "Hey, you're a big guy. What are you about 6' 3" and 500 pounds? Maybe 520? Are you wearing a flimsy Teddy under your overalls as you look at that Chevy Truck? And what color is your Teddy? (Chances are it's red). Red is the most popular Teddy color then comes black and then white. Me? I like a nice maroon color Teddy but I have yet to see one in a big mans size. (The maroon people refuse to make Teddys in that color bigger than a medium. I have written them many times on this. And shown them a picture)

I usually go to a certain Teddy store in the Mall that I like: The sign in window said:

"ARLEE KOPLUNKOWITZS
BIG MANS TEDDY STORE"

And then in a smaller sign underneath it:

"NOT AFFILIATED WITH LEE PLINKOWITZS
BIG MANS PANTY STORE"

This was in the Crestview Mall where I shop. (Cumberland County) I like they way they treat you there and they have a nice selection of XXXL and XXXXLLLL Teddys to fit any big man.

Plus Arlee comes out of the back and ruffles out the Teddy on several big men as they step in front of the mirror to admire themselves. I once bought a Teddy and paid him in walnuts.

I like Arlee's commercials which I have seen on TV. I like when he says: "Find a Teddy cheaper from any of our competitors and I will drop my pants for youuuu!" I like when he says "youuuu" at the end of the sentence like he just keeps going with the word until he runs out of breath.

And then one of his salesman in the commercial brings over a customer who found a Teddy cheaper and Arlee looks at the man's receipt and says: "Just like my commercial says. I will drop my pants for youuuu." And then he does. He stands in the crowded store and drops his pants for the camera. He is a man of his word.

So it was my Korean wife's surprise (and mine too) that I was told that Arlee Koplunkowitzs Big Mans Teddy Store in the Crestview Mall was closing after 41 years. And another store was taking its place. Their sign on the window said:

"THE TEDDY BARGE"
"BIG MANS TEDDYS AT BULK PRICES.
BARGE PRICES!"

I read the ad under the sign: "If you wear a size 50 and up see us first. If you want a Teddy that fits you right—see us first! If you like a nice selection of colors in Big Mans hard to find colors see us first! If you just want to be around other big men in sheer wispy lingerie see us first! We know you have many choices when it comes to big man's lingerie but after you shop around all the Teddy stores in the Tri Area-Tri Region-Tri Section Triangle come on in, get fitted, have a mocha, and let us give you a real good Teddy fit. The Teddy Barge! Extra large Teddys at really small prices Men only, please. No browsers. No Maroon!"

Well, I thought. Competition is always good for both businesses. I mean Cumberland County must have 32,000 big men living there and almost all of them wore big mans panties or big mans Teddys. I wondered if I would shop at the new place.

My Korean wife, Sun Chuc Du, and her Eskimo friend, Huong Tin Twan, were busy looking at the broken fountain in the Mall as I wondered whether to go onto The Teddy Barge. Could I change?

My wife always seemed to stare wistfully at a cascading fountain that was broken or a fire hydrant that had blown. Our marriage was solid. "Sun Chuc Du!" I called out but she just looked at that fountain. Then she dove in. I paid a man in pimentos to fish her out.

I was in the Mall looking for a book called "Gus The Field Goal Kicking Turtle" which was about a turtle that kicked field goals for a Turkish Football team who smoked a lot of cigarettes. I did not find it. (The book).

I like to relax to the "Gus The Turtle" series of books of which there are many. The last GOOD one I read was "Gus The Ecstasy Taking Turtle" which was about a party turtle and his adventures with girls. Another good Gus book is "Gus Gets A Plastic Surgery Makeover." This is about a turtle who changes his appearance and the doctor who put him though a 12 hour surgery.

I tire now. No more of this story.

COMPLETIO

CUMBERLAND COUNTY
SHOE STORE

"YES WE HAVE TRIPLE WIDE SIZE 3 MENS SHOES!!!"
screamed the sign in the window. That's what they
pushed at this shoe store. Yet no one in town wore a size
3 mens shoe let alone triple wide. I once asked the owner
why he had that sign in the window if nobody bought the
shoes. And he said, "That's why we have them. Because
nobody bought them." I guess that made sense in a
strange way. But I have to admit he was right. LARRY!!!

Cousin Junie owned the shoe store in Cumberland
Country. We had only the 1 shoe store in town owned by
this large happy man (Cousin Junie.) He was nobody's
cousin but that was his name on his birth certificate. But
everyone just called him Sweetie.

"SWEETIES TRIPLE WIDE FEET"

was the name of his shoe store. Junie, Sweetie, Cousin—
the man had 9 names, what was the point? Call yourself
a name and stick with it.

Well let me tell you that the good citizens of Cumberland County were upset. And they had a right to be. One
shoe store and they specialized in triple wide shoes in the
size 3-5 range? For men? Women did not have a shoe
store in town and had to buy their shoes through the
mail.

Sweetie was a strapping man of 6 foot 5 inches with a
shock of wavy red hair. They called him Shock in the
Navy, he once told me. (After his hair) Sweetie would
sometimes take me down to the woodshed and show me
Navy welts on his back. He said he got them from sailors

who would hit him with straps during lights out games. I never knew what Sweetie meant by that. But who was I to ask? Sweetie was a nice man that never really wanted to sell shoes but just got into it. He said he just wandered into this particular field. "It could have been goats. It just happened to be shoes," he told me once. "I didn't care," he said. "Goats, shoes, it's all the same."

He had a big red beard, with a shock of red hair like I said and big red bushy eyebrows. Aunt Flayleen once said to him—"Sweetie, why don't you shave some of that red hair? You don't need all that red hair all over your face. In fact you look like an idiot." But he never did shave all that red disgusting hair. That was Sweetie. (The idiot)

I once went in the backroom of this shoe store and saw: Six pairs of broghams, Hush Puppies, some Thom McCann tassel loafers, a pair of Espadrilles, boat sneakers, 19 gladiator sandals, and beach thongs. All very small. Maybe up to size 5 and a half. I wore Espadrilles and flip flops throughout high school. (Cumberland High).

Well, men needed shoes so they had to shop at Sweetie's shoe store. There wasn't much of a selection and Sweetie was all sweaty most of the time with the running back and forth from the backroom then trying tight small shoes on men's feet and all that disgusting red hair and beard with food in it in the way. There was always maybe 15 or 20 men in the shoe store at any one time. All walking around doing the shoe walk admiring their shoes and cramming their feet into his footwear and standing in front of the mirror asking, "How does this look?" And "What do you think of these?" I think I may have seen some panties peeking out. I know I saw a teddy.

And Sweetie would always say. "How do they feel? That's the most important thing. How do the shoes feel

on your feet? Are they too tight? Let me pinch your
toes." And he would always grunt to get down on the
floor, all 6 feet 5 of him and pinch those toes in those
tight shoes. He must have pinched 75 toes a day. That's
what I thought. He said "Are you crazy? Let's say each
man has an average of 9 toes on his foot and there are
65 men in the store every day. That's 585 toes a day
times 7 equals 4,095 toes a week!" (He counted on his
hands.) "I should close on Sunday," he went on. "That'll
save me 585 toes I got to pinch!"

His stock wasn't so great and the store was old and
musty. And there was a permanent blueberry smell in
there. It could have been blueberry then again it could
have been boysenberry. I was usually pretty good with
jam smells in old musty shoes stores but this one
stumped me. But you needed shoes, you needed shoes.

That was our shoe buying experience in Cumberland
County. "Sweeties Triple Wide Feet." OTTO!!!

umberland county college

February 25, 2004

Mr. Edward Broth
10153 1/2 Riverside Dr. # 241
Toluca Lake, CA 91602

Dear Mr. Broth,

I recently received a copy of the short story you wrote that you sent to Cumberland County College for submission in either our newspaper or Literary Magazine. Unfortunately, we do not accept submissions from anyone who is not a member of the campus in either publication.

The Student Newspaper is published as part of the Journalism courses and is completely produced by students. The contents of the paper is limited to news articles written by students to given them the experience of writing in a professional setting.

grape
jelly
stain
(or could be strawberry)

I am sorry that we can't help you and want to thank you for your submission.

Sincerely,

Cumberland County College

BIBB COUNTY SHOE STORE

COMING SOON! said the sign. And it wasn't soon enough for the good residents of Cumberland County. With only 1 shoe store in Cumberland another shoe store the next county over was a welcome relief.

MENS SHOES! was the sign underneath the COMING SOON sign.

This was cause for celebration. I mean after 13 years people were sick of Sweetie and his shoe store. They gave Sweetie dirty looks and disgusting glances and a few took a punch at him. One man wrestled him to the ground in his own shoe store and held him there until another threw a Hush Puppy at him. Another tried to grab clumps of his disgusting red hair off his head. "I'm sick of you and that red hair. You look like an idiot," he said.

If you remember, Sweetie owned the only shoe store in Cumberland County. It was called "SWEETIES TRIPLE WIDE FEET" and they only sold mens shoes. This went on for 13 years.

So! A NEW shoe store right within driving distance in Bibb County—well, people couldn't wait. I mean the tension level was ramped up to 5! This was almost road rage tension. People even stopped shopping at Sweeties store in anticipation of the grand opening. Even though they needed shoes. Who needed Sweetie and his stupid shoe store anymore?! That's all people talked about. "We won't have to deal with Sweetie anymore! A new Shoe Store is opening! For our convenience!"

And then the new store's sign went up:

"SWEETIES TRIPLE WIDE FEET"
NOW IN BIBB COUNTY!

And underneath that:

CLOSING OUR CUMBERLAND COUNTY STORE!
HOPE TO SEE YOU AT OUR
NEW STORE IN BIBB COUNTY
THANKS FOR SHOPPING WITH US
THESE PAST 13 YEARS
SHUTTLE SERVICE AVAILABLE

Sure the drive was long. But they had shuttle service. Sweetie at least had a van to shuttle people from Cumberland County to Bibb County to shop at his new store. If you wore a triple wide shoe size 3–5.

CRICKET MAGAZINE GROUP

Dear Author:

Thank you for your interest in our magazines and for submitting your manuscript(s) for our consideration. My editorial staff and I have carefully studied your material, and we regret to inform you that we do not find it appropriate for our publications.

We are glad to have had this opportunity to see your work, and hope that you will be successful in placing it elsewhere.

Sincerely,

Editor-in-Chief
Cricket Magazine Group

Babybug°   Ladybug°   Spider°
Cricket°   Cicada°

Stories of
Love
and
Encouragement

THE HUG STORE

The "HUG STORE" opened in the Mall today. The sign on the window said:

NEED A HUG?
COME ON IN. WE HAVE ALL KINDS OF HUGS!
(NOT AFFILIATED WITH
THE BURLINGTON COAT FACTORY)

I went in. There were pictures on the walls of the various kinds of hugs they offered for sale: A man getting a bear hug, a woman getting a hello hug, a grandmotherly hug given to a young boy, a soldiers hug to another soldier, a phony show business hug, and so on. I didn't see anything that really caught my attention and the store was kind of empty except for one fat guy with a red beard getting squeezed. I looked on the wall and noticed he was getting the Vietnam Veterans Hug, a popular military hug for ex serviceman. The store was located next to a Vermin's Restaurant in the Clearview Mall. (Cumberland County) I usually took my lunch there. I enjoyed a stuffed mosquito crunch with a crab appetizer. That was enough for me. I am petite. I think I have mentioned before but I am 5 foot 1 inch 102 pounds. (No boils.)

The clerk behind the counter said he would be with me in a few minutes. I looked around. The big guy with Oak Ridge Boy beard finished his hug, shook off some beige flakes from his beard, paid the clerk, took some brochures and left. "Now can I help you?" said the clerk.

I said I was looking for a hug. He laughed and said everyone who comes into the store was looking for a hug. He said "What kind of hug was I looking for?" I told him I didn't know. He said let me show you our hug catalog. He thumbed through his catalog with me. There were the same pictures that he had on the wall. Plus a lot more. He explained them to me. "This is our Texas Bear Hug. Very popular. It's a big bold hug that says, I gotcha now." I told him that I thought I was not looking for that kind of hug. That it was too much of a hug. He said he understood, it's not for everyone. He flipped through the catalog some more. "Now here's our California Hug. It's a lighter airier hug that is more of a greeting. It says 'Hi. How's it goin'? Nice to see ya'. And it comes with avocado."

I told him I was a little depressed and I was looking for a hug that simply said everything is going to be OK. I told him I just wanted a hug that said 'Hey, you're doing a good job, you count.' I asked him what the big bearded guy got. He called out to his hug associate: "Hey, Sherry. What was that hug you just gave to that big bearded customer with the dirty beard?" She said it was a squeeze, as she finished eating her sandwich. I believe the sandwich had some pimento in it as I distinctly saw some red dots.

I said wasn't that the Vietnam Vets Hug I saw on the wall? She nodded her head "no" and said it was a squeeze. She was very definite about that. Why do I think people are lying to me?

The clerk said that was his lunchtime special: A squeeze for five dollars. He said a squeeze was still a hug but that they could discount a squeeze but the price was set for a hug by the manufacturer. I said I needed more than a squeeze. He laughed and fluttered his eyes like a bird. I thought I saw a Spaghetti O come out of his mouth and land on me. But I didn't want to look down. Neither one of us wanted to look down but we both knew that a Spaghetti O flew out of his mouth and landed on me. Some things in life you just know. A Spaghetti O landing on you is one of them.

I chose the <u>Standard Hug</u>. He said he needed to check on that. He went behind the curtain then came back. He told me they were out of that hug. It was very popular. That it was on special order. Did I want to wait? I told him no! Waiting is for fools. He called out to the hug associate again. "Hey Sherry, when is the Standard Hug coming in?" She said they discontinued that hug; it was a 1017 hug, no longer manufactured; it was completely out of stock and they could not reorder. He said "Shows you what I know. I didn't even know the Standard Hug was discontinued." Then he belched out a plum. We both looked at this purple thing on the linoleum; his eyes fluttered.

I was tired of this place and this man. I just wanted my hug and to get back to my shopping in the mall. (For the record I was looking for a shirt with a flap that went down to my tassels. So far I was unsuccessful. Perhaps I would try Flap World. They advertised "Yes, we have shirts that have flaps that go down to your ankles. However, they were out of the one in the ad.)

Finally I told him that if they were out of the hug that I wanted I would come back to the store at another time. And that right now I was going to finish shopping in the mall. He said he understood, was very nice about it, and told me to come by anytime and that he would try to accommodate me. Service was their business. I left the store and blended into the people in the mall.

WORSHIP
L E A D E R

August 16, 1999

Dear Worshipper.

Thank you for your article entitled "The Hug Store." Were that I had unlimited pages to share with our readers, I would slate everything that comes to my attention. There are indeed many things that would be interesting and deserve a greater audience.

That being said, since I do not have unlimited room, I am afraid that we will not be able to publish your piece. Please feel free to contact us, however, with any other ideas that you have. Our editorial schedule is always in need of fine-tuning and we are interested in hearing from those in the field.

Thank you for your continued support of Worship Leader magazine.

Blessings,

Worship Leader magazine
Editor

THE PAT ON THE BACK STORE

It had been a while since I was at the Clearview Mall. However, I needed to buy some fake hair for a party that I was having that day and I was also edgy so I decided to go to "THE JUMP ROPE STORE" and get some jump roping in. Bill "William" Pilaf and his family ran the place and I had known all of them since birth. I know there were a lot of jump rope stores to choose from but I always liked this one.

Inside the mall I wandered over to "The Hug Store." I thought today was a good day to get a hug so I went inside. I remembered the owner and went up to him. He was busy looking at a picture of a sailor sitting on a rock in the sun. I said I was thinking of getting a hug today. He said they were no longer The Hug Store. He said people in town did not respond to hugs. They did not want them; had no use for them. They were not selling. He said they were now "THE PAT ON THE BACK STORE." He pointed to a sign he had up:

NEED A PAT ON THE BACK?
COME ON IN.
WE HAVE ALL KINDS OF PATS ON THE BACK!
(NOT AFFILIATED WITH BURLINGTON, VERMONT)

He pointed to some pictures on the walls of various people getting different kinds of pats on the back. They looked like the same people in the photos from The Hug Store. There was the Texas Pat On The Back. A woman getting a hello pat on the back, a grandmotherly pat on the back given to a young boy, a soldiers pat on the back to another soldier, a phony show business pat on the back, and so on.

He said people in this town wanted pats on the back and that is why he changed his store. I said that made sense. He told me that almost everyone that came into his old Hug Store said, "You know I'm not in the mood for a hug but if you sold pats on the back I would buy that. So I changed over." I stifled a noise.

He said what kind of pat on the back was I looking for? I told him I didn't know; I was expecting a hug not a pat on the back. He said let's look through the catalog and once I saw the many pats on the back he offered he was sure I would find some pat on the back to my liking. I yammered and spit out a sesame. It was beige. It landed on the linoleum. We both looked at this beige seed on the linoleum; his eyes fluttered.

The Pat On The Back Store manager showed me the same binder. This time there were pictures in there of different people getting pats on the back. He said, "Now here's our Texas Pat On The Back. Very popular. It's a big bold pat on the back that says, I gotcha. It says you're doing a good job and we're proud of you." I told him that I thought I was not looking for that kind of pat on the back. That it was too robust, too much of a pat on the back. He said he understood, "It's not for everyone." He flipped through the catalog some more. "Now here's our California Pat On The Back. It's a lighter airier pat on the back that is more of a greeting. It says 'Hi. How's it goin'? Nice to see ya'. And it comes with avocado."

I said "No." It was a firm no, I remember that.

He continued flipping through the catalog and said "What about this one? This is our Continental Pat On The Back. It just came in. Very popular already. It's more like a French pat on the back. More of a slap."

I told him I liked the good old fashioned American Pat On The Back. He seemed snippy at that like I was ordering regular coffee at a Starbucks. I made a mental note to hate him.

He said "What about our Standard Pat On The Pack then? That's $25.00 for 5 minutes of steady patting on the back. It's just a no frills pat on the back and it's for when you're feeling a little low, more of a pick me upper. No slapping, but it's a solid pat. We don't hold back. It's a full pat."

Then he called out to an associate. "Hey, Sherry, how many of the Standard Pat On The Backs do we have left? She said she would find out for him. She disappeared through a curtain and when she came out she said they discontinued that model and the new model was coming in, possibly that Thursday. She said that was model #1005B and that the manufacturer no longer made that model, it was discontinued, something about a faulty part that stung people when the patting started. He said, "Shows you what I know. I didn't even know they discontinued that pat on the back. And I'll bet my dog ran off with a cat."

I was tired of this place and this man. I just wanted my pat on the back. Finally I told him that if they were out of the pat on the back that I wanted I would come back to the store at another time. And that right now I was going to finish shopping in the mall. Maybe buy a pretzel. He said he understood. He told me to come by anytime and that he would accommodate me. He gave me a partial smile, I gave him a semi half nod.

Once again I left the store and blended into the people in the mall. I think I saw a man in a gorilla suit buying a candle at a kiosk.

WORSHIP
L E A D E R

September 30, 1999

Dear *Worshipper*

    Thank you for your most recent submission, "The Pat on the Back Store." Unfortunately, this does not fit our editorial needs at this time.

    Worship Leader magazine seeks to inform and educate church leaders in the development of church worship. Familiarizing yourself with our editorial content is the first step in establishing a working relationship with a magazine.

    God bless you as you continue to serve Him with your writing.

Blessings,

Worship Leader magazine
Editor

THE WALK YOU TO YOUR CAR STORE

I had been in the Clearview Mall (Cumberland County) last Wednesday to shop for a gift. I was looking for a commemorative silver serving dish called the ARTHUR ASH TRAY, memorializing Arthur Ash the great tennis player, when I decided that what I really needed was a pat on the back. I was feeling low and I thought that would lift my spirits. So I walked over to the Pat On The Back Store in the Mall. (Clearview.) I got to the store but the sign on the window was changed. It said: Now Open! "THE WALK YOU TO YOUR CAR STORE"

NEED A WALK TO YOUR CAR?
COME ON IN
WE HAVE ALL KINDS OF WALKS TO YOUR CAR!
(NOT AFFILIATED WITH BURLINGTON INDUSTRIES)

Why had they changed the store? I went inside. The owner said the Pat On The Back Store did not sell. He said that after an initial surge of business that people did not show up anymore. "They just did not want pats on the back. I couldn't give them away. I must have ordered 300 pats on the back and sold maybe 20 of them. Sure, at first we did rush business. Everybody wanted a pat on the back, especially after 9-11, but then it slowed down and there was little repeat business." I saw medical dribble come out of his ear. He told me almost everyone that came into his Pat On The Back Store said, "You know, I'm not in the mood for a pat on the back but if you sold walks to the car I would buy that." "So I changed over." I blew a piece of veal onto his shirt. I noticed a magazine he was looking at with a picture of a fireman in just suspenders and big rubber boots sitting on a ladder. I said "How much?"

He said that depended on what time of day, where my car was in the mall parking lot, and how busy he was, and what kind of walk I was looking for. "Here let me show you what kind of walks we offer": He pointed to some pictures on the wall of various people getting walked to their cars. They looked like the same people in the photos from The Pat On The Back Store. There was the Texas Walk To The Car. A woman saying hello while getting walked to her car, a grandmotherly walk to the car with a young boy, a soldier being walked to his car by another soldier, a phony show business walk to the car, and so on.

"Let's look through the Walk You To Your Car Catalog," he said to me and he pulled out a binder. I was suspicious. This looked like the binder that contained the pat on the back pictures. "Now this here, this is a Texas Walk You To Your Car. Very popular. It's a big bold walk that says, I gotcha. It says you're doing a good job and we're proud of you. That's why I'm walking you to your car."

I told him that I thought I was not looking for that kind of walk to my car. That it was too robust, too much of a walk, too quick paced. He said he understood, "It's not for everyone." He flipped through the catalog some more. "Now here's our California Walk You To Your Car. It's a lighter airier walk that is more of a jog. It says 'Hi. How's it goin'? Nice to see ya' when you pass others walking. And it comes with avocado."

I said "No." There was no hesitation. I remember that. He continued flipping through the catalog. Some pictures of weight lifters in bicycle shorts tumbled out. They had grunt faces on. He scooped them up and put them back in the binder. "What about this walk to your car? This is our Brisk Midweek Special. It just came in. Our Walk Attendants will take you to your car, up to the B Parking Lot for $17.00. And if you give them a ride back, you take $3.00 off that price." I noticed many customers talking to the Walk Attendants getting ready to be walked to their cars. The Walk Attendants were wearing walking clothes, comfortable shoes, and had white pith helmets on. They also carried sunscreen, bug spray, and power bars. (Dee-licious!)

The store constantly had a sign in the window: "Be Back In 5 Minutes"

I told him I liked the good old fashioned American normal walk to your car. "You know, a nice walk out of the mall, where I don't fumfer around in the parking lot forgetting where I parked." He laughed and shook his head. "That certainly is a big seller he said, let me even see if we have that in stock." He called out to a clerk behind the counter: "Hey, Sherry, how many of the American Normal Walks To Your Car do we have left?"

She said she would find out for him. She disappeared through a curtain and when she came out she said they discontinued that walk and the new walk was coming in, possibly midweek. She said that was walk #HC50 and that the manufacturer no longer made that walk, something about a faulty part that tripped people up when the walking started. He said, "Shows you what I know. I didn't even know they discontinued that walk. And I'll bet my wife ran off with a man in a gorilla suit."

He said "What about our Standard Walk You To Your Car? Just until the new walk comes in. That's $20.00 for 15 minutes of steady walking. Until we find your car. It's just a no frills walk. No chatting, just a solid walk. We don't hold back. It's a full walk."

I told him I would think about. I said "Thanks, let me give you a hug." He said he was out of that business.

I was tired of this man and his walk talk. I left and blended into the mall. I think I saw a man dressed like a radish.

The Cumberland Observer
CC SF

Monday, December 8, 2003

ACROSS THE STATE

ECONOMY

Greenspan Approved for Fifth Fed Term

Interest rates on short-term Treasury bills continued to surge, reflecting investors' expectations that the Federal Reserve will raise its benchmark short-term interest rate soon.

The Treasury sold $17 billion in three-month bills at a discount rate of 1.39%, up from 1.23% last week and 1.13% the week before. An additional $15 billion·
bills at
1.505%
week b
The
the act
1.413%
with a
$9,964.
month
In a
said t
year
sury
dex fo
justab
to 2.0
the pr

EAR
GM F
Fore

Ge
affirm
target
money
that r
hurt i
opera
GN
autor
its 200
$2.25 a
quarter this year and $7 a share for 2004, excluding special items, GM Vice Chairman and Chief Financial Officer John Devine said.

Net income fell to $22.2 million, or 44 cents a share, from $23.2 million, or 46 cents, a year earlier, the Orrville, Ohio-based company said. Sales in the quarter ended April 30 declined 1.1% to $325.4 million, the first drop in more than three years.

Mortgage Application
Index Slips 8.9%

between compensation under the 2001 law and the 1973 Rehabilitation Act, which prohibited discrimination by those receiving financial assistance from federal programs.

THE ECONOMY

30-Year Mortgage Rates Rise to 6.32%

The average rate on a 30-year mortgage climbed to 6.32% this week, Freddie Mac said, amid investor expectations the

The larceny charges are part of an overall case by prosecutors that accuses the former executives of looting Tyco of $600 million.

But Obus did throw out half of the charges against Kozlowski in a separate case that accuses him of cheating on taxes relating to art purchases.

TECHNOLOGY

AMD Plans Launch of Dual-Core Chips

The Southeast Asian nation of-

Some analysts had expected Lockheed to be selected for the program, which might be worth $20 billion.

CalPERS Raises HMO Premiums by 11.4%

The California Public Employees' Retirement System as expected adopted health plans

appear to have taken $9 billion in advance deals for the 2004-05 broadcast season.

The Mortgage Bankers Assn. said its gauge of loan demand dropped to 568.8 from 624.6 the week earlier. The group's refinancing index fell 14% to 1,363.2, the lowest since the week ended April 19, 2002. Purchase applications also fell.

RAILROADS

Union Pacific Lowers Earnings Forecast

Boeing said it would supply modified versions of its 737-800 passenger jet outfitted with advanced computers and other electronic gear from Raytheon Co., Northrop Grumman Corp. and Britain's Smiths Group. CFM International, a joint venture of General Electric Co. and France's state-owned Snecma,

Also

Cash-balance pension plans are designed to even out company pension contributions over an employee's career, unlike traditional plans in which benefits are calculated based on length of service and highest salaries earned.

While cash-balance plans have won praise for allowing workers to transfer earned benefits when they change jobs, some argue they discriminate

SQUIRREL CAMP OPERATOR ARRESTED

Camp was a disease pit say Police.

by Lou Snyder
Herald Staff Writer

Police took into custody earlier today Leon Fedgermann, 57, owner and operator of LEON FEDGERMANN'S SQUIRREL FANTASY CAMP on charges of grand theft. "It seems Mr. Fedgermann was training squirrels to steal jewelry and wallets and other valuables from the fantasy camp he operates near Flotsam Woods," said District Attorney, Roy Bludge. "This had been going on awhile now and after a careful investigation Mr. Fedgermann was apprehended without incident at his camp about two o'clock this afternoon and taken in." Police confiscated over $300,000 worth of jewelry reported missing from a host of camp-goers. "I've never seen so much squirrel disease," said police officer Donald Ouch. (No relation to Deputy DA Ronald Ouch). "Squirrel waste everywhere. It was disgusting."

THIS MORNING

I made a doody this morning and it winked at me. I could not believe it. I looked at it and I distinctively saw it wink at me. That is something. I told my teacher this story. I take a summer school course to learn spaghetti making and am doing nicely. To date I have made some very nice spaghetti. I've showed it to others.

I continue with my story titled: THIS MORNING.

Then I noticed my doody was bunching together and when it was all bunched together it looked like Ben Affleck. At first it didn't, but then when it all moved together it had the face of Ben Affleck. My doctor told me this was very common. "Many stools look like Ben Affleck," he said. "Many people have come to me and told me their stools looked like Ben Affleck. It's nothing to be concerned about. If your stool looked like Al Pacino then you should worry because Al Pacino is a ruddier stool."

I felt good that I had this doctor. He said that a stool that looks like Al Pacino can be a sign of a more serious problem. That it was a rubicund, more grayish, older look-ing stool. There was an elderly lady who passed away at Glendale Health Hospital and her chart said: Deceased. Elimination was a soft Al Pacino looking sample.

Yesterday I took a picture of this stool and sent it to Ben Affleck and told him that my stool resembled him. But I have not heard back yet. Maybe it is so common that many people have told him that their stool looks like him. He must be a very busy man. I heard Ben Affleck doesn't take crap from anyone.

Some other things I told my doctor this morning. I have been ordering underwear from a Hunter's catalog for some time. I like catalog underwear better then buying it at a store. I usually try it on with the mailman waiting so: The mailman can see if these underwear fit properly. The mailman can usually give you a pretty good fit with your mail order undies. If you let him. Yesterday, I got some Hunter's underpants delivered. And let me tell you—these are very nice underpants. They fit very nicely. I tried them on in the foyer in front of my mailman and showed him how the elastic waistband was snug and how I could move properly in the leg holes. He agreed. I saw him scoop up a handful of hard candies that I keep in a dish in the foyer but I did not care. Hey, he's: 1. My mailman 2. Showing me how my underwear fits.

What do I care about a few root beer barrel hard candies?

Ed Broth
10153 1/2 Riverside Dr.
#241
Toluca Lake, CA 91602

Dear Ed:

We at GRIT Magazine thank you for allowing us to read your submission, *This Morning.* Unfortunately, because of space limitations, the interests of our readers, and the large volume of articles offered to GRIT, we often must return good work.

The confidence you express in GRIT through your submission means a great deal to us. We believe our readers are our most successful contributors and will continue to make GRIT a publication that conveys the best of American life and tradition.

GRIT's old-fashioned appeal and good news approach means we are always looking for well-written articles — with heart – accompanied by several excellent quality color photos. Please study current issues of the magazine for guidelines.

What did I eat?

Perhaps you will have another submission that will be perfect for GRIT. Good luck in your writing efforts.

Sincerely,

Editor in Chief

ED BROTH
10153 ½ Riverside Dr.
#241
Toluca Lake, CA 91602

Editor
GRIT MAGAZINE

Jul 10. 2003

Dear Grit Editor

Thank you so much for reading my work titled: THIS MORNING.
And thank you for calling my submission "good work". I knew it
was! Because you mention Grits old fashioned appeal and good
news approach and you say you are always looking for well
written articles and you asked if perhaps I had a another
submission . . . Well I do. I am now sending it to you.

Unfortunately I don't have any excellent quality color
photographs like you asked for. (They did not come out in color)
However, I may be able to draw you a picture. Say what does
"Grit" mean anyway? I looked it up and got: some stuff that gets
stuck in other stuff. As in when there's grit in stuff. It gets stuck
in there. I admire that you have a magazine for this when others
don't. Hey, are those potato chips for your sandwich or mine?

Now down to my submission—my companion piece to THIS
MORNING. (Enclosed) I hope this meets your needs for publication.
I hope it has the good old fashioned appeal you are looking for. The
best of American life & tradition you are seeking. I am working on
taking a picture but need just the right moment.

With Respect,

Ed Broth

Ed Broth

LATER THAT AFTERNOON

I called my doctor. I was alarmed. I had gone to the bathroom again to make a doody. I now noticed that when my
stool bunched together it looked like Matt Damon. My
doctor immediately instructed me to come to his office.
Within an hour I was sitting across from Dr. Goopta. Dr.
Sinji Goopta. Now let me tell you here about Dr. Sinji
Goopta. Dr. Goopta specializes in celebrity stools and is
also an animal chiropractor. Many times I have brought
my turtle in to him for a shell realignment. In his native
Sri Lanka he has also reattached conjoined twins that
were tired of calling into the next room to talk. He was
an expert.

"This is a more serious problem," he said. "A stool
that resembles Matt Damon is a cause for concern. More
tests are needed. I am prescribing Zolon. There may be
side effects such as runny nose, abdominal swelling, and
trumpet type noises." The doctor had a chart of various
foods that he pulled down. It made a flapping noise. "The
foods that you eat can lead to your elimination looking
like Matt Damon. A combination of, say, radishes and
Bologna will do it. Or maybe you are eating a lot of
Sesame dressing. Or sesame bread sticks. We have seen
this as a cause."

I said "How do you get my stool back to looking like
Ben Affleck?" Ahhh, he said, that is why medicine is so
mysterious. Then he offered me a Dot. This is a gel like
candy that comes in many colors. I enjoyed a green one.
He devoured them like a baboon at feeding. "Stay here,"
he said and he left his office. I immediately licked all of
his tongue depressors then put them back. When Dr.
Goopta returned he said that he would run a series of
tests with his associate Dr. Goopi and get back to me. I

told him I was nervous and anxious and that I felt something was wrong. "All I can do for you now is validate
your parking," he said. "Do you have a ticket?" That is
my story.

AMERICAN LIFE & TRADITIONS

September 8, 2003

Ed   Broth
10153 1/2 Riverside Dr   #241
Toluca lake   CA   91602

Dear Ed

Thank you for your interest in GRIT. We appreciate your manuscript submissions. Unfortunately, they do not suit our needs at this time.

We are enclosing a copy of our Guidelines For Writers and Photographers.

Please feel free to send us other submissions.

Sincerely,

The Editors

        Later That Afternoon

I LOVE DOGS

I bought a dog from the Pound today. I wanted to start the new 2003 year right. This was my first time at the Dog Pound and I did not like the smell. My dog is very nice though. It is gray with one blue eye. I took it home and I decided to call my dog John Wayne. I like this dog very much. It itches itself a lot but that's OK. It looks just like John Wayne.

I had a dog before. It was part Great Dane, part Chihuahua. It had the body of a Great Dane and the legs of a Chihuahua and the walk around the block killed it.

I came home from work Saturday (I repair novelty gags) and I saw my dog on the couch licking himself. He was really going at it. Really licking down there. I said to my wife, "Why is John Wayne licking himself? He's all red down there." She said she was trying to get him to stop. I told her to try some more.

John Wayne used to get up on my lap and lick my face until I could take no more. Then I took more. John Wayne licked his yohos one day for 3 and ½ hours while my entire family ate a spaghetti dinner. No one seemed to care. My uncle said, "Is John Wayne licking his garbanzees again?" I said "Yes" and we went about our business.

A few days later we decided to get another dog so we would have two dogs. So we went back to the same Pound and this time I picked out a dog with one gray eye who was blue. I had never seen a blue dog before but this one was. This is a very nice dog and I like it very much. It is playful and sometimes drinks a lot of water. Yesterday it regurgitated some of the meatball that I fed it.

We immediately named this dog Maurice Gibb (of the Bee Gees). It looks just like Maurice Gibb—sad watery eyes with a droopy face. I think it may be a Basset Hound. Well, let me tell you these two dogs got along wonderful. They play and have fun and chase each other around. Yesterday I came home and there were these two dogs locked in an embrace. They were really locked tight. Their eyes were bulging. I said to my wife "Why is Maurice Gibb humping John Wayne?" She said she tried to get them to stop. I told her to try some more.

My uncle said, "Maurice Gibb is really sc*e*ing the hell out of John Wayne, isn't he?" I said he was. Then my uncle regurgitated a meatball from dinner the night before. It was very funny seeing my wife trying to separate John Wayne from Maurice Gibb with all that panting going on. What fun we had.

I Love Cats Magazine
c/o Editor Lisa Allmendinger
16 Meadow Hill Lane
Armonk, NY 10504
908-222-0990
908-222-8228--fax

1/18/03

Dear *Ed.*

Thank you for sending me your story but the style/content is just not appropriate for the audience of I Love Cats Magazine.

Thank you for thinking of I Love Cats Magazine.

Sincerely,

Lisa M Allmendinger

Lisa M. Allmendinger
Editor
I Love Cats Magazine

Where's the cat in this story? Did I miss Something?

ED BROTH
10153 ½ Riverside Dr.
#241
Toluca Lake, CA 91602

Editor Lisa Allmendinger
I LOVE CATS MAGAZINE
16 Meadow Hill Lane
Armonk, NY 10504

1/28/03

Dear Editor Allmendinger,

Thank you for reading my story "I LOVE DOGS". I sincerely appreciate it. And for pointing out to me that there was no cat in the story. I must have forgot to send you the correct version: "I LOVE DOGS BUT LET'S FACE IT—I REALLY LOVE CATS" story. It's loaded with the "cat" that you are seeking. I hope you like it. It's a more sensitive story—more suited for your magazine. I think. (cleaned up a bit for the cat audience)

Respectfully,

Ed Broth

Ed Broth
Really a cat lover

I LOVE DOGS BUT LET'S FACE IT—I REALLY LOVE CATS

I bought a dog from the Pound today. **They were out of cats!** I wanted to start the new 2003 year right. This was my first time at the Dog Pound and I did not like the smell. My dog is very nice though. It is gray with one blue eye. I took it home and I decided to call my dog John Wayne. I like this dog very much. It itches itself a lot but that's OK. It looks just like John Wayne. I had a dog before. It was part Great Dane, part Chihuahua. It had the body of a Great Dane and the legs of a Chihuahua and the walk around the block killed it.

I came home from work Saturday (I repair novelty gags) and I saw my dog on the couch licking himself. **Cats don't do that!** He was really going at it. Really licking down there. I said to my wife, "Why is John Wayne licking himself? He's all red down there." She said she was trying to get him to stop. I told her to try some more. **I said, "I wish we had a cat. They're more intelligent! So unlike dogs.**

John Wayne used to get up on my lap and lick my face until I could take no more. Then I took more. John Wayne licked his **cahoobas** one day for 3 and ½ hours while my entire family ate a spaghetti dinner. No one seemed to care. My uncle said, "Is John Wayne licking his **mahahee's** again?" I said "Yes" and we went about our business. **Cats don't do that!**

A few days later we decided to get another dog so we would have two dogs. So we went back to the same Pound and this time I picked out a dog with one gray eye who was blue. **They were still out of cats. (But they were on order).** I had never seen a blue dog before but this one was. This is a very nice dog and I like it very much. It is playful and sometimes drinks a lot of water. Yesterday it regurgitated some of the meatball that I fed it. We immediately named this dog Maurice Gibb. It looks just like Maurice Gibb—sad watery eyes with a droopy face. I think it may be a Basset Hound. Well, let me tell you these two dogs got along wonderful. They play and have fun and chase each other around. Yesterday I came home and there were these two dogs locked in an embrace. They were really locked tight. Their eyes were bulging. I said to my wife "Why is Maurice Gibb **fidgeting** John Wayne?" She said she tried to get them to stop. I told her to try some more. **I said "Cats wouldn't do that. They're too intelligent! They just make a noise!**

My uncle said, "Maurice Gibb is really **pl*wing** the hell out of John Wayne, isn't he?" I said he was. Then my uncle regurgitated a meatball from dinner the night before. It was very funny seeing my wife trying to separate John Wayne from Maurice Gibb with all that panting going on. What fun we had. **Cats are great! I love them!!!!**

I Love Cats Magazine
c/o Editor Lisa Allmendinger
16 Meadow Hill Lane
Armonk, NY 10504
908-222-0990
908-222-8228--fax

3|2|2003

Dear Ed:

Thank you for sending me your story but I have already published a manuscript that is similar in theme or topic to the one that you submitted.

I am booked at least a year in advance with stories at this point.

Thank you for thinking of I Love Cats Magazine.

Sincerely,

Lisa M. Allmendinger

Lisa M. Allmendinger
Editor
I Love Cats Magazine

The Tampa Herald

THURSDAY, AUGUST 14, 2003

Retail Sales in July Exceed Forecasts

the percentages of cuts or when they would go into effect.

The text has been handed to the heads of delegations at the World Trade Organization in Geneva, less than a month before trade ministers are set to meet in Cancun, Mexico.

The 1.4% increase is the largest in four months. U.S. report indicates consumer spending remains robust.

in four months. The department also revised upward the results for May and June.

The strong retail sales results for July indicated that consumer spending, the largest element in economic growth, was holding up relatively well even as the rest

and financing deals.

Retail sales excluding motor vehicles rose 0.8%. Sales surged 1.2% at appliance and electronic stores and were up 1.3% at garden center and hardware stores. However, sales dropped 1.5% at retailers of sporting goods,

Spending upswir

U.S. retail sales, seasonally adju
(in billions)
$325 ················· $3

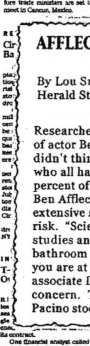

AFFLECK STOOL IS SIGN OF SERIOUS MEDICAL PROBLEM

By Lou Snyder
Herald Staff Writer

Researchers now say that human waste that bunches together to form the image of actor Ben Affleck is a sure sign of a serious medical problem. At first doctors didn't think this was a serious medical problem but after examining 3,216 males who all had a celebrity stool after elimination the Affleck stool was present in 86 percent of those tested. Celebrity stool specialist Dr. Sinji Goopta says that the Ben Affleck stool at first was thought not to be a medical risk. However, after extensive studies and analysis the Affleck stool has been upgraded to a level 5 risk. "Science is not an exact science," Says Goopta. "We did further extensive studies and exploration and we are now convinced that when you go to the bathroom and your stool bunches together with the face of Ben Affleck in it, then you are at serious medical risk." "It's still not the worst though," says, his associate Dr. Menohar Goopi. "That's still the Al Pacino Stool that is the biggest concern. That is one you you want to stay away from. Very few survive a Pacino stool. It is deadly."

Affleck Stool

---

its contract.

One financial analyst called the change the first major blow to Overture since it said it would merge with Yahoo Inc.

The company, which still expects second-half profit of $2.40 to $2.50 a share, said same-store sales would be in the range of a 1% drop to a 1% increase. Federated said earnings this quarter might fall to as low as 25 cents a share and fourth-quarter profit might rise to as much as $1.29.

Shares of Federated fell 37

An Overture spokesman said the company was disappointed by T-Online's decision and called it a contract breach.

From Reuters

WORKPLACE

Supercuts to Settle Bias
Suit for $3.5 Million

1.4% from the previous month to $317.2 billion, according to a preliminary tally by the Commerce Department.

STRONG RESULTS: *Second-quarter sales were below expectations at were strong at the retailer's warehouse unit, Sam's Club.*

Sam's Gives Wal-Mart

The warehouse unit shows strength amid a price war. Overseas sales also contribute to the retailer's earnings surge.

From Reuters

Wal-Mart Stores Inc. said Wednesday that its quarterly earnings rose nearly 21% as strong results from its Sam's

The biggest increase was reported in motor vehicle sales, which rose 3.2% from the previous month as consumers took

Costco warned last week that its quarterly profit would miss expectations.

Selling the bank-card business could free up cash for its retail business, in which same-store sales fell 8% in June and July because of a drop in customer traffic, lower prices and disruptions from remodeling, Circuit City said.

Shares of Circuit City dropped 5 cents to $9.50 on the Wal-Mart Chief Executive Lee Scott said he had not ex-

up
while
to g
R

lysts on ·········· were expecting a profit of $2.06.

Wal-Mart quarterly sales increased 11.3% to $62.6 billion, while sales at stores open at least a year — a key retail measure —

cent
erni
by ?

able
the
high
cast

stou aau earnings this quarter might fall to as low as 25 cents share and fourth-quarter profit might rise to as much as $1.20.

Shares of Federated fell 3 cents to $42.84 on the New Yo

Stories of
Meaning
and
Sacrament

MY TALK WITH DADDY

My Daddy called me up the other day and asked me if I knew the difference between a hundred nickels and a hundred nipples. I said "No."

He said "No one wanted to see his collection of Buffalo nipples."

I told my Daddy that I thought that was disgusting and that I did not care for that kind of humor and that I did not want to hear it anymore.

A few days later Daddy called me up and asked me if I knew the difference between a bag of nickels and a bag of nipples?" I said "I did not."

He said "Then come out to the car because I want to hit you over the head with something."

I said that once again "I did not care for that kind of talk and that I thought he was disgusting and that I was going to hang up for now."

This morning—It was Tuesday, December 2002—and I was cleaning a rubber band out of my nostril when my Daddy called me on his cell phone. He had 62,000 unused minutes and was dialing wildly. "I may have called Spain and made a dental appointment," he told me. Then after telling me about a food that did not agree with him (he said it was not a food that gave him a stomach ache—but rather a food that just did not share his same political views)—he asked me "If I knew the difference between one nickel and one nipple?"

I said "I did not."

He said "The difference is he never put a nipple in a parking meter. At least not on purpose."

We both had a big laugh over this; the time he accidentally stuck a nipple in a parking meter in San Jose and did not get time on the machine. And his car was towed and he head to walk home. And the parking meter was broken from that nipple in there. We really laughed and reminisced about this. Then I threw a paint filled balloon at my neighbor's full clothesline. Frank Tint makes me nauseous.

I like my Daddy and his sense of humor.

Ambassador
Magazine

January 3, 2003

Ed Broth
10153 ½ Riverside Dr. #241
Toluca Lake, CA 91602

Dear Mr. Broth:

Thank you for submitting your story "My Talk with Daddy" for publication in AMBASSADOR Magazine.

Although it is extremely well-written and interesting, our lineup for the foreseeable future is already set and we will be unable to accept any more articles.

I am returning it to you along with a list of other Italian American publications that might be interested in running it.

Thank you again for thinking of sharing this article with us. I enjoyed reading it and urge you to keep seeking to publish it. Recording our past is extremely important, as well as a worthy and essential endeavor.

Congratulations on producing such fine work.

Yours truly,

Kevin Heitz
Editor

cc: Elissa Ruffino

Ambassador Magazine – A Quarterly Publication of the National Italian American Foundation
1860 – Nineteenth Street, NW • Washington, DC 20009
TELEPHONE: (202) 387-0600 • FAX: (202) 387-0800

Ed Broth
10153 ½ Riverside Dr.
#241
Toluca Lake, CA 91602

Mr. Kevin Heitz, Editor
Ambassador Magazine
1860 19th St. NW
Washington, D.C. 20009

Jan 15, 2003

Dear Editor Heitz,

I once knew a Garvin Hentz, I wonder if you two are related. First
of all, thank you for reading my work: "MY TALK WITH DADDY".
And thank you for saying such nice things that it was extremely
well written and that you enjoyed reading it and that it is
extremely important recording our past as well as a worthy and
essential endeavor. I agree. I am encouraged. (I showed others
your flattering letter around here after our afternoon shower &
medication and everyone was very happy to see it.) I have sent
"MY TALK WITH DADDY" to everyone on the list of over 100
names that you gave me of other Italian American publications.

    I am now enclosing a new story: "MY CAR RIDE WITH
DADDY". It includes MANY REFERENCES to the Italian American
experience and recording the past. I hope you like it.

    Please encourage me more and let me know if I am indeed on
the right track.

With Sincere Respect,

Ed Broth

Ed Broth

MY CAR RIDE WITH DADDY

Daddy had just bought a new 2003 Pontiac Penne Gorg-onazola with insurance money he made when he slipped in a Loomanns and took a rack of Big & Tall dresses down on him (crushed hernia). And was giving me a ride home. He said to me "Do you know the difference between a fat man's ass and an alarm clock?"

I said "I did not."

He said "One has 2 hands on it and the other—when it makes a loud noise in the morning—get out of bed!"

I told him I thought that was the most disgusting thing I had ever heard and that he was disgusting and that I was ashamed of him. This coming from an 88 year old Caucasian man. I was truly ashamed. And so were most Italians.

A little while later Daddy said to me: "Do you know the difference between a fat man's ass and a puppy?"

I said "I did not."

And he said "One I once saw splashing in the toilet and the other I gave your mother for her birthday but it pooped on the carpeting."

I told him that I thought that was disgusting and that I did not think it was proper for a father to tell a son those jokes anymore. I told him I could not believe what I was hearing, that he was truly disgusting, and that joke was disgusting. I told him that I was dismayed and that I hoped he had the good taste not to tell that joke in mixed company. (Near Italian women) And that as his son, I was embarrassed for both of us. He was pathetic. (For an Octavegan)

Daddy was pulling onto the driveway in his insurance bought Pontiac Penne Gorgonazola when he said to me, "Do you know the difference between a fat man's ass and a stop sign?"

I told him "I did not."

He said "One is round and has red in the middle of it and the other is virtually on every street corner in Philadelphia." Home of Justin Guarini. From American Idol.

I told him "Yes, that is true—there's a fat man on virtually every street corner in Philadelphia with all their cheese steaks, and hoagies, and pretzels and walk away sundaes. And yes a fat man's ass is round and red in the middle.

We both had a good laugh and I told him I thought he was clever to come up with such a clever joke and that I was glad he told it to me. I said this was very entertaining and that he really had something here and that I enjoyed my talks with him and that I was glad he was my Daddy. I love Italians!!!

I like my Daddy and his sense of humor. I belched up some melon.

Ambassador
Magazine

January 29, 2003

Ed Broth
10153 ½ Riverside Dr. #241
Toluca Lake, CA 91602

Dear Mr. Broth:

Thank you for your kind letter and the submission that accompanied it. I shared your story, "My Car Ride with Daddy," with a few people in my office, and it was well received. As far as publication in AMBASSADOR Magazine, I think it is a little too short. We normally publish stories that are 1,000 words or more.

I am enclosing the most recent issue of the magazine, as well as a tile that the NIAF had made for our 2002 Annual Convention and Gala.

Thanks again for the submission.

Sincerely,

Kevin Heitz
Editor

Ambassador Magazine – A Quarterly Publication of the National Italian American Foundation
1860 – Nineteenth Street, NW • Washington, DC 20009
TELEPHONE: (202) 387-0600 • FAX: (202) 387-0800

Ed Broth
10153 ½ Riverside Dr.
#241
Toluca Lake, CA 91602

Mr. Kevin Heitz, Editor
Ambassador Magazine
1860 19th St. NW
Washington, D.C. 20009

Aug 11. 03

Dear Editor Kevin Heitz,

Thank you very much for reading my new story. And thank you
for sending me the tile. I took it in the shower area and many
admired it. One wanted to hold the tile for more then the allotted
65 seconds. But I did not let him! Why should I? It is a very nice
tile and I will use it appropriately. I will cherish it forever or at
least until I move and have to pack things up. One fella here said
he knew a Crevin Hinimintz and wanted to know if you were him.
Are you?

Now down to my latest submission. 1,000 words is certainly a
lot of words. However, this NEW story should have that many. If
you don't count a word twice. Like I use the word "The" many
times. Is that one word or 15 words? Thank you for helping me.
Like they say, you are good people. I sincerely appreciate that you
take time out for me. I have told many workers here.

I am a long time reader of Ambassador Magazine. It is the
finest magazine about ambassadors out there. I am now submitting
my story. I hope you like it. You are more then an ambassador.
You are a consul.

Sincerely,

Ed Broth

Ed Broth

MY BUNGEE JUMP WITH DADDY

Daddy was on the bridge ready to throw himself off with a long rubbery thing on him when he said to me "Do you know the difference between a Boxer dog and Boxer Shorts?"

I said "I did not."

He said "One is brown and white and laying on my bathroom floor right now and the other I threatened my landlady with."

I told him I thought that was disgusting, one of the most disgusting things I had ever heard, not a nice thing to say to a son, and disgraceful. I was ready to jump over the edge with Daddy. We finished attaching our harnesses and rubbery things and we jumped off the bridge.

On the way down Daddy said to me: "Do you know the difference between a rectal thermometer and a Christmas tree?"

I told him "I did not."

He said "One, when I finally get it up, my eyes pop out. And the other, your mother told me to shove up my ass the night before Christmas."

I told him "I thought that was appalling and vulgar, rowdy and obnoxious. How can you tell a son that? It's course, salty, crude and unpleasant and should not be told to a son. I was affronted and disgusted" as we dangled in the air. "Furthermore," I said, "It's an affront to me your son, my mother, and our Christmas tree. I made a Fiddle Faddle greps. We flew through the air and bounced around. Daddy's ears flapped.

Daddy was boinging in the air on that rubbery thing and I was boinging next to him when he said to me, "Do you know the difference between an engagement ring and a baboon's butt?"

I said "I did not."

And he said, "One I gently eased onto your mother's finger and said marry me. And the other your mother got mad at me because it got stuck on her finger at the zoo."

I told him "Yes, that is funny. Enjoyable humor. I loved my Mamma but it would be comical if you eased a baboon's butt onto her finger and it got stuck there. (Especially during a wedding proposal) I told him I'm sure that has happened before with zoo personnel especially veterinarians who do examinations and lose a ring. Yes I was amused." I love my Daddy. We dropped to the ground. Frank Tint is a bastard.

MEELEE WOBBLE'S
SWIMMIN' HOLES

That was the name on the Swimmin' Hole business. "Formerly Rickey Blobby's Swimmin' Holes". Before MeeLee Wobble took it over.

Rickey Blobby sold the Swimmin' Hole business to MeeLee Wobble one summer and everyone wondered how that would affect the swimmin' hole trade. (For the record there were 12 swimmin' hole companies in Bibb County. Rickey Blobby's was the biggest and some say the best) MeeLee Wobble was Uncle's Cleto's friend. They hung around and I think it was Uncle Cleto who introduced MeeLee Wobble to Rickey Blobby.

The new name of the business was "MEELEE WOBBLE'S SWIMMIN' HOLES".

MeeLee would build the swimmin' holes in his warehouse and then send them to you and install them in your backyard. They were big with the grass and shrubs and the actual water hole and they measured 1200 feet long and 3600 feet wide and to this day I don't know how he got them built and sent to each customer but he did it. He may have sent it UPS. He was always talkin' about the men in the brown shorts and how they did him wrong and how he'd like to steal something from them for spite. "I'd take a stick to those brown shorted Ba* ar#s if they didn't have my credit card number," is what he would yell from his window to anyone approaching.

MeeLee was a Hawaiian gentleman and he always wore a grass skirt, no shirt, and barked at a coconut head in his truck on his lunch break. He also wore a shower curtain ring in his nose. He was a real fixture in town. He had enormous toes. He would count on his toes in his truck as he ate his lunch. (Burger King. Every day) Many remarked: "That MeeLee sure has some big toes. Don't believe I've ever seen toes that thick and wide before". But nobody would tell him that to his face. (He looked like Lyndon Johnson and on a few occasions was mistaken for Hitler.)

Once the swimmin' hole arrived in the brown truck (that parked just about anywhere it wanted) he would take about 20 minutes and the swimmin' hole would be installed in the backyard of your house and you would have a swimmin' hole ready for the summer where you could splash around, have some horseplay, throw rocks, go fishin' and dive in. He sold about 20,000 of them in tiny Bibb County. And out of the 20,000 only 2 gave anybody any trouble. (An alligator ate a dog in one and quicksand gobbled up a family in the other) Other then that MeeLee Wobble's Swimmin' Holes was good product.

IT'S YOUR BUSINESS

August 27, 2003

Ed Broth
10153 1/2 Riverside Dr. #241
Toluca Lake, CA 91602

Dear Mr. Broth,
We appreciate your interest in submitting your short story to our magazine.
Unfortunately, any interest we would have in the fiction arena would be that which is
directly related to the professional pest management industry.

Sincerely,

Managing Editor
Pest Control magazine

ED BROTH
10153 ½ Riverside Dr.
#241
Toluca Lake, CA 91602

Managing Editor
PEST CONTROL MAGAZINE

Jan 13, 2004

Dear Editor

Thank you for reading my story and pointing out to me that
there's nothing in there that's related to the pest control industry.
After re-reading my story I have to admit you are right. I must
have left out the pest control. With all my re-filing and re-crossing
and re-indexing and re-referencing I made a mistake.

    Not to be a pest, but I would like to submit to you a NEW story.
This one I'm sure meets your needs. It is loaded with pest control.
It's got exterminators in it and bugs and sprays; enough pest
control for everybody.

    I hope you like it. Thank you again for considering my short
story for your magazine. I read your magazine all the time. And
enjoy it very much. It gets passed around quite a bit here.

Respectfully,

Ed Broth
Future Pest Control Industry Employee

MY DAY WITH DADDY
THE PEST CONTROL MAN

Daddy is an exterminator. He works for HARRY S. TRU-MAN PEST CONTROL. Their motto is: "THE BUG STOPS HERE". And Daddy was driving his pest control Volkswagen with the big mouse ears and the rat tail and I was sitting next to him. He was going to spritz some bugs when he said to me "Do you know the difference between an Italian flag and a brassiere?" I said "I did not."

He said, "One I waved proudly over my head at a German soccer game. And the other my granddaddy tried to make a slingshot out of."

I told my Daddy that I thought that was disgusting and I did not care for those kinds of jokes and that I was embarrassed at this type of conversation as Daddy sprayed and spritzed some creepies. He was really spraying and spritzing those bugs. Daddy continued driving in his mouse exterminator VW on the way to extinguish some Tetramorium Caespitum when he said to me "Do you know the difference between a cowboy hat and a sanitary toilet seat cover?"

I said "No."

He said "One you pop up the top, put on your head, and you're ready for line dancing. And the other I got so drunk once I put on my head and everyone said I looked like Garth Brooks."

I said "That is disgusting, I don't want to hear it, it's offensive, you are offensive, and this kind of talk is revolting. Not for a son to hear. Not from his Daddy." I was appalled.

Daddy got out of his car and spritzed and sprayed some more. A few Nacerdes Melanura Linnaeus fell over dead. While he was putting the offender mites in a plastic bag he said to me "Do you know the difference between a water fountain and the musician Pete Fountain?"

I told him "I did not."

He said, "One dribbles and spittles. And the other . . . if you get too close, it will wet your shoe."

I told Daddy, yes, I thought that was funny. And yes, Pete Fountain, the Dixieland clarinet player—he could dribble and spittle with his clarinet. And if you got too close to him he may wet your shoe. But certainly a water fountain would too. I thought that was enjoyable humor, suitable for all, and that water fountain humor and wet-ness was just plain good funny. I love my Daddy. He makes me laugh.

Daddy staggered from the pest control fumes. But he was OK.

HONOLULU HANK

Honolulu Hank was in town. And that was always a cause for joy. Honolulu Hank was a former carnival act that just danced around on his own. He would stand in a vacant lot and wiggle around and charge admission to this. There was no other people in the act, no horses or trained bears or clowns or fireworks or anything else. Just him. I don't know why but he sure did draw the crowds. Upwards of 12,000 people would come to that vacant lot whenever Hank was there wiggling and jiggling. He was 62 years old. He lived in Hawaii and he talked about how he played for millions all over the world. Just in Honolulu clothing wiggling around. What an act!

Honolulu Hank from Honahakiki, Hawaii. That's how he billed himself. And he would stand in a field with a hula hoop and his Hawaiian costume and do his act. Sometimes 17 people showed up, sometimes 6 people, sometimes 12,000 people. He would still do the same show for 3 people or for 15,000.

Here's an excerpt of his show: Used with permission—Honolulu Hank@2002.

"I'm Honolulu Hank from Honahakiki, Hawaii and I stand here and hula hoop for your enjoyment. Enjoy me swiveling. Come in close ladies and gents while I swiggle from side to side. I am 62 years old. You say you don't know what swiggling is? Well just watch me move from side to side with my Hula Hoop on. I'm Honolulu Hank From Honahakiki, Hawaii. Watch me swiggle. I've got my Hula Hoop on and I'm from Hawaii. Watch me spin around in the vacant lot. I've got my shirt off. Come on around. The more the merrier. My name is Honolulu Hank."

This went on for 6 hours and 45 minutes. People would yell requests, bring lawn chairs, stay all night, but he would just do his act. No matter what they wanted him to do he would just swiggle. "I'm Honolulu Hank from Honahakiki, Hawaii and I stand here and hula hoop for your enjoyment Enjoy me swiveling. I am 62 years old." He said it over and over again.

And the people would be fascinated. I mean amazed. No one left. Oh sure a few fainted and needed medical help and had to leave and one woman gave birth there in that field but that was it. He would stand there in that empty field and do his show.

He stopped doin' his act on that field when they built a swimmin' hole. Biggest job MeeLee Wobble ever had. When it was finished, he started up his act again. What memories.

LOG HOME LIVING

August 21, 2003

Ed Broth
10153 1/2 Riverside Drive, #241
Toluca Lake, CA 91602

Dear Ed,

Thanks for submitting the story about Honolulu Hank. I enjoyed reading it but unfortunately we don't have a place for this kind of writing in Log Home Living. I hope you can find another magazine that runs these types of articles so you can see it in print.

Best regards,

Editor-in-Chief
Log Home Living

LUAU LESTER

Luau Lester came to Bibb County. He was in town. And the people were excited. Luau Lester was an entertainer who stood in a vacant lot and did his act. Well, let me tell you the people loved this Luau Lester. He wore a grass skirt and swayed from side to side moving his arms in a wavy motion and holding a fire stick as he roasted pig on a spit. The people watched. He was formerly from Hawaii.

There was no one else in the act. Just Luau Lester in a big vacant lot. But the people sure did come. As many as 12,000 would stand there and watch Luau Lester sway and move his arms and rotate his pig. "I'm Luau Lester from Lakakani. That's off the island of Lanamini. Come and watch me sway and turn my pig around on the spit. I've got a fire stick. I'm here for your entertainment. Gather around folks. I'm 61 years old. You say you don't know what swaying is. Then come and watch me. I'll show you what swaying is. Come and gather around. Plenty of room for everyone." That's what he would say as he did his act. This went on for 6 hours and 45 minutes. He just stood there in that empty lot and moved his arms in a wavy motion and swayed. What swaying!

Well one day Honolulu Hank was doing his act in a vacant lot for around 10,000 people and all of a sudden Luau Lester showed up. He said nothing; just set up his act in the other vacant lot across from Honolulu Hank. Then he started: "Come on around ladies and gents. Watch me sway. I'm Luau Lester from Lakakani. I have a grass skirt. What's under it? Wouldn't you like to know. Maybe grass underwear? I'm 61 years old. I have a fire stick. That's my pig I move around. I have no shirt on. Those are my chest hairs."

As soon as Luau Lester started his swaying and pig turning and wavy arm moving, the people stopped watching Honolulu Hank swiveling and turned their attention to Luau Lester. Then they all left Honolulu Hank and walked across the road to the vacant lot that Luau Lester was in. "Come on around and watch me sway. Gather in folks. I'm here for you. I have a fire stick. I'm Luau Lester from Lakakani."

Well, all Honolulu Hank could do was watch. Watch Luau Lester take his audience for the full 6 hours and 45 minutes. He just stood there the entire time and watched this Luau Lester sway and move his fire stick and turn his pig. No one turned around to see Honolulu Hank that day. Not a person. They were all watching Luau Lester. Hank was not impressed with the act. What memories we had.

Bulletin of the ●
At⊙mic
Scientists

February 18, 2004

Ed Broth
10153 1/2 Riverside Drive #241
Toluca Lake, CA 91602

Dear Mr. Broth:

Thank you for providing the editors with an opportunity to review your manuscript,
"Luau Lester." Unfortunately, it has been decades since the *Bulletin* adopted a policy
of not printing fiction or poetry. Therefore, the piece is unsuitable for the magazine at
this time.

Again, thank you for thinking of the *Bulletin*.

Very truly yours,

Editor

ED BROTH
10153 ½ Riverside Dr. #241
Toluca Lake, CA 91602

Editor
Bulletin of The Atomic Scientists

Feb 23, 2004

Dear Editor

Thank you for reading my story "Luau Lester." I am an avid reader of the Bulletin of The Atomic Scientists. I have read the magazine from cover to cover for a long time and rarely if ever, if even more rarely, miss an issue. I pass your magazine around to others here and they also rarely, if ever, do not enjoy it. (It is rare). Let me just say that "Luau Lester" is a real person not a fiction story. However, I can understand you may not want to publish it in your magazine.

I want to take this opportunity to submit a new story to you which is "Honolulu Hank". Also a real person.

I really like The Bulletin Of Atomic Scientists. My Daddy was a scientist and his Daddy before him was a scientist (Atomic). Atomic scientists run in our family. So . . . we have a lot of this atomic scientiscism around us. I am not a scientist. However. But I like your magazine. It's in Daddy's visor now in his car. I saw it earlier there.

Please consider my new story—"Honolulu Hank" for inclusion in The Bulletin Of Atomic Scientists. Once again, "Honolulu Hank" is a real person, thus a real story—not fiction or poetry. Although I do have poetry if you want to see that.

Thank you, Ma'am, for considering this and I want to say you have a great magazine there. All of us here try to get it out of Daddy's visor when he parks and visits Charlette.

Respectfully,

Ed Broth

Ed T. Broth
(Future Scientist (Atomic)

*the*American Scholar

Dear Mr. Broth

This will acknowledge receipt of your manuscript:

LUAU LESTER

We should forewarn you that because all pieces that are being seriously considered are read by at least three editors—who may have to wait until the closing of the next issue—you can expect a careful but, alas, not a swift reply. Thank you for your interest in *The American Scholar*.

The Editors

TO: AMERICAN SCHOLAR
From: ED BROTH

I am taking "Luau Lester" out of the hands of The Bulletin Of The Atomic Scientists. This should really be in American Scholar. I studied Spanish in school. Hola!

THE AMERICAN SCHOLAR

March 31, 2004

Ed Broth
101531 Riverside Drive, #241
Toluca Lake, California 91602

Dear Mr. Broth:

I'm writing to report that, after careful consideration, our decision has been against taking your essay "LUAU LESTER" for publication in *The American Scholar*. Because of the number of manuscripts we receive, we are unable to comment on rejected articles. Many well-written and interesting pieces are turned away because we can publish so few essays a year.

We appreciate your letting us consider this piece and hope you find a place for it elsewhere.

Sincerely,

Managing Editor

BIBB COUNTY ELECTIONS

What a campaign! Bibb County was the center of attention as two gubernatorial candidates came from this small county to battle it out for Governor.

Rudy Delapeep decided to run for public office. "I'm out of the rubber man business," he told voters. "I don't want to be a carnival contortionist anymore. You want to see me contort then come to my campaign speech. I can bend myself there. Rudy Delapeep is your twisted man. I'm the rubber brother." That was his announcement on KFLT, the local channel. And the people came. Almost everybody in Bibb County, The Wash Up Town, came to his campaign speech announcing his candidacy. He kissed babies, shook hands, handed out dish towels, smelled sexy ladies—all the while putting his body through a series of twists and bends and curvatures to the delight of the crowd. "I don't know how he does it,"

marveled Honolulu Hank who happened to be in town in an open field Hula Hooping when Rudy swung by to deliver a speech and a contort. "He has over 27 bends," said Honolulu Hank. All I do is swivel. Come and see me swivel ladies and gents. I swivel for your enjoyment." One lady whispered to me, "I can see your Uncle Rudy's garbonzas* dancing around when he stands there with his leg behind his ear holding his campaign sign."

Rudy Delapeep gave 65 speeches in 3 days. He blanketed this small burg with his views on everything from gun control, to the economy to jobs in the wash up business. "If elected, I will see that every man, woman and child in America, every car that travels our highways, every tourist and visitor on the road will come to Bibb County to gas up, get a Pepsi, and throw away trash. That's my promise to you! Rudy Delapeep for Governor!" Then he put his feet over his head, balanced on his hands, and spoke to the people with his face between his legs.

"You're talkin' through your butt," said his opponent, Paul Zee, an Asian business owner who was smart, classy, experienced, and a well funded politician who was on course to be President. He held up his campaign signs: "You Want Paul Zee!" "Paul Zee Makes Everything Good!" "Paul Zee For You!" Aunt Flayleen said to me "It sounds like Palsy." And I said, "But that's his name! Paul Zee."

"Yeah, well who wants to go around saying "You want Palsy. And Paul Zee Makes Everything Good?" I politely dislodged a small piece of nectarine from inside my mouth and Aunt Flayleen saw me discharge it onto the sidewalk. We both looked down at this sliver of orange on the cement. That was our afternoon.

Paul Zee set up his campaign headquarters next door to the Foo King Restaurant. And he went on television and told the people: "Anybody who believes the competitive spirit in America is dead hasn't been in a supermarket checkout line lately. So come by my campaign office and say hello to Paul Zee and then go next door to that Foo King restaurant." People were confused. "What's he talkin' about?" said Andy Milk, a local. And "I know he's smart and articulate and owns the public laundry but I just like that damn rubber man better, "said Mel Sillee, another local."

Art "Arthur" Sandwich was Rudy's campaign manager and he along with his assistant campaign manager, Ham Johnson, ran, I must say, a solid campaign. He got the dog vote early on and that proved to be the difference. There were 1,032 dogs in Bibb County and they won the right to vote in 1977. (You may remember Art Sandwich who had written the Book "Chuck Tetito— Prison Husband.")

Rudy had all the great entertainment at his campaign parties. He got all the stars to come out and support him. He even got the old 1930's cowboy singing star Ko Tex to make an appearance and sing a song on his horse. The girls liked that. Parrot Top performed. This was the comic bird with the orange wig who yells out jokes and has props.

Paul Zee was trailing badly in the polls. He did everything to convince the people to vote for him. His last gasp effort was his promise: "I will wrestle an alligator in a UPS outfit." But it was too little, too late. He lost. Paul Zee lost the race and Rudy Delapeep became Governor of Bibb County. The vote was 93 percent for Rudy Delapeep, 5 percent for Paul Zee, and 2 percent skim milk. Rudy Delapeep was the new Governor of Bibb County. One lady told me "I saw your Uncle Rudy's ping pongs* hoo hah-in up and down when he gave a speech while on his hands." And Daddy said, "What do you want me to do? Say something to Rudy? Older men at the beach show the same thing. Live with it. He's a contortionist. That's my brother. Now he's Governor."

I tired now. I don't want to write this anymore. I go to sleep.

---

*puka beads

www.thebark.com

August 25, 2003

Dear &.i.

We are very grateful to you for thinking of The Bark in connection with your work. I regret having to send you this disappointing news, but we are very sorry that we are unable to use it. Being a quarterly magazine, our space is very limited.

Because we receive many submissions we are unable to respond to each with individual letters. But we certainly wish you the best of luck and appreciate your interest in our magazine.

Best wishes,

Editor

*Stories of
Spirit
and
Courage**
**Plus Windshield
Flyers*

OCTAVEGAN DATING SERVICE!

MEET NEW PEOPLE
GET ACQUAINTED

MEET OTHER OCTAVEGANS FIND LOVE
THEY ARE OUT THERE AND WANT TO
MEET YOU!

(Not affiliated with Burlington Industries)

If you are an Octavegan—someone who is is 1/8th Vegetarian, 1/8th Carnivore, 1/8th Dairy eater, 1/8th Putz, 1/8th Cuban, 1/8th Creole, 1/8th French, 1/8th Filipina, 1/8th Caucasian, 1/8th Hawaiian and want to meet a mate JUST LIKE YOU call us. WE WILL MATCH YOU UP!

1-800-Octavegan
(Not affiliated with the Burlington Coat Factory)

We will match you up with other 1/8th people! Meet the 1/8th Vegetarian, 1/8th Carnivore, 1/8th Dairy eater, 1/8th Putz, 1/8th Cuban, 1/8th Creole, 1/8th French, 1/8th Filipina, 1/8th Caucasian, 1/8th Hawaiian person of your dreams! They're out there! And they want to meet YOU!

ATTEND OCTAVEGAN EVENTS. DANCE WITH AN OCTAVEGAN. FIND ROMANCE. EAT BREAD. GET A NEW MORTGAGE. YES WE HAVE PENAL EXTENSIONS.

OCTAVEGAN SINGLES MIXER THIS SATURDAY!
BIBB COUNTY OLIVE GARDEN RESTAURANT
(Formerly The Moist Mule Restaurant)
Win a stuffed pepper for your lady!

BACK TO THE DRAWING BOARD
OF ED BROTH

To: The United Methodist
      Publishing House

For: Mature Years Religious
     Magazine

Please accept my submission to your magazine

"The Further Adventures Of The Funny Cartoon   By Ed Broth
UH, OH I JUST CUT OFF MY TOE"

"Uh, oh, sweet Mother of God, Good Lord Our Savior
in Heaven, Good God Almighty, I just cut off my toe."

Publisher and
Distributor
for the Church

February 4, 2003

Mr. Ed Broth
10153½ Riverside Drive, #241
Toluca Lake, CA 91602

Dear Mr. Broth:

Thank you for letting us consider your material. We regret that it does not fit into our present plans for publication and that we must disappoint you by declining it.

Furthermore, careful consideration of your work makes it apparent that it is unlikely to ever meet the stringent publishing guidelines and standards of *Mature Years* magazine. We do not advise additional submissions of your work.

We regret that the large volume of submissions does not allow time to comment on each piece or to personally respond to the many enclosed letters.

Cordially,

MATURE YEARS magazine
THE NEW INTERNATIONAL LESSON ANNUAL
DEVOTIONAL COMPANION TO ILS

TEENIE'S SISTER KITTY

Teenie's sister Kitty came to visit for Thanksgiving. Kitty was Teenie's fatter sister. Teenie was 247 pounds and Kitty was 328 pounds and she always sat in her big stuffed leather chair with her cat which was also named Kitty. She loved that cat. What a sight to see Kitty and her cat Kitty. Around the holidays when the 2 sisters and the 2 pets got together you had Teenie and Teenie and Kitty and Kitty. They all kinda had the same face. Kitty, the heavier sister, had some hairs growing out of her upper lip. So did the cat. Once I yelled out to Kitty's stepfather: "Kitty's lying on top of the TV and she won't move." And her stepfather yelled back, "Which one?"

And I yelled back, "Does it matter?"

And he yelled back, "Yes. If it's Kitty the cat it's OK. But if it's Kitty, my fat daughter, then get her off the TV. That fake wood bends."

Kitty

Kitty

I must say Kitty looked fabulous this visit. She was now living in Aqua Velva, Colorado where she was a masseuse. Her slogan was "Free Massage. Just Buy A Pretzel." I had not seen her in years and she was up to 328 pounds. Her shoes collapsed under her weight. They burst open like a melon. The sides just gave way. She told me she was now 16 pounds heavier then her car. She looked at her Miata registration and noticed it. I told her that I had recently picked up Plumpers Magazine and she was hot!

Now Teenie and Kitty's stepfather, Gene, had remarried. He married a woman named Jean. I must admit there was some confusion when Kitty would yell from the backyard: "Gene!"

And Kitty's stepfather would yell back, "Which one?"

And Kitty would yell back to him, "Does it matter?"

Gene   Jean

And he would yell back to her, "Yes! If it's G-e-n-e, then it's me. If it's J-E-A-N then it's your stepmother."

Teenie's stepfather confided in me one day about his new bride, "The reason I love her is when were having sex and I have to leave the room for any reason—she stamps my hand." I nodded a nod of agreement he gave me a head tilt of accord.

Gene had a saying he would always say about the Gassy family. "Were not quitters. We may be stopperers, lie downerers, take a breakerers, but we're not quitters." I smelled fudge on his breath. But it could have been radish. I am usually good at identifying food smells on senior's breaths but this one stumped me.

What a holiday dinner! Mamma's sister, Ardetta Finchfry Broth, a circus roustabout at age 86, cooked for everybody. She was in that hot kitchen for 15 hours straight. Just her. She wouldn't let anyone else in. I peeked in and saw her with a doo rag on her head, her eyes bulging out like a driven over frog, and a face full of squinch. "You hot in there, Ardetta?" I said to her.

She just looked at me and yelled out: WILL SOMEONE DEFOG MY WINDSHIELD!! Then she collapsed. Went down like Janet Leigh in the Psycho shower curtain scene. Pulled 3 curtain rings down on her and laid there with just the one eye glazed over. I declined to step into the room.

The meal was spectacular. Chicken and turkey and beets and salad and buttered rolls and coleslaw and yams and pumpkin pie. Later on we found out it was take-out from Popeye's Chicken when we saw 312 cartons in the garbage. I was suspicious when I saw Popcorn Turkey as the main course.

Then after dinner we all went to the family room where everybody played bongos. There were 64 of us playing bongos. Yet not one neighbor complained. Gene regaled us with stories of his days as a horse owner. He told us he invested in a horse once named Gaysex. He said the horse was a winner. Then he bought a horse named Queerbait, sold it to a telemarketer, and then left the horse business altogether after getting a mysterious rash on his palms. Now he works at Fat Mans Clapping Haircutters where he is employed as a senior stylist.

Ardetta Finchfry Broth wandered into the room, turkey stuffing and cranberry pellets smeared all over her face. Although groggy, She made it to the end table lamp then yelled out "WILL SOMEONE UNCLOG MY DRAIN!!" Then she went down. Collapsed like a folding card table. (In 3 swift motions).

The holidays are always a good time to reminisce. Sure some people have bugs around this time but what's a few insects among relatives. I'm glad we had a chance to see our family. Teenie and Teenie and Kitty and Kitty and Gene and Jean. What holiday fun! My bandaid fell off.

COMPLETIONIO

Gene   Jean   Kitty   Kitty   Teenie   Teenie

Bead&Button.

February 27, 2004

Ed Broth
10153 1/2 Riverside Dr. #241
Toluca Lake, CA 91602

Dear Mr. Broth,

Thank you for considering *Bead&Button* for publication of your short story, "Teenies Sister Kitty". I did not find the story in the envelope. It sounds like the story may have fit the Anything Goes page but the editors have decided to eliminate that page. Therefore, we will not be able to accept your story.

Sincerely,

Editorial Assistant

The Cumberland Observer   Monday, December 8, 2003

BOB FORTIN   FORTIN' AROUND

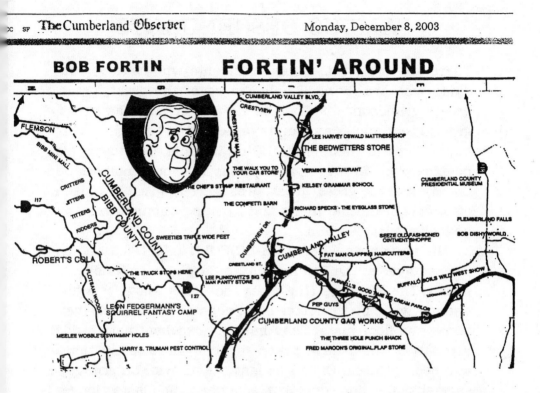

WELCOME ONE AND ALL!!   HOPE YOU ENJOY TODAY'S COLUMN!

I may be talkin' out of line but Larry King is gorgeous... I think I'm addicted to 2nd hand smoke...Who's an Octavegan in Bibb County? No, it's not Gene Gassy...My secret is out. I smell...Had dinner the other night at Vermins Restaurant. Stop in and see Ray the former disgraced Pep Guys manager. He let a car fall on an old lady. Now he's in his diaper at the front of the new restaurant in the Clearview Mall seating people. Ray - I won't drop my lawsuit against you. You're a cork soaker (wine sommelier) with your filthy hands. The blood of many is on you. Your head waiter Maurio is back from his double amputee operation and good as new. He fell into some pudding in the kitchen when he leaned the wrong way but luckily the diners didn't see it...Say what you want but my Ford Festiva still attracts police women when I slow it down...The new Sock N' Shoe Restaurant opened in the Mall yesterday. Try their Saki and Shoeshi. (Delicious wine and raw fish on rice)...

"FAQ YOU" (FREQUENTLY ASKED QUESTIONS)

Why is there 29 pieces of pita bread to a package but only 18 falafel balls to a package?...That's it for now. Ran out of space. It's me - I'm Bob Fortin - Fortin' Around

FAMOUS DESCENDANTS

There are many famous ex-presidents who have descendants who are living. I have heard of the great, great,
great, grandsons of Thomas Jefferson and the great,
great, great uncles and aunts of Benjamin Franklin living
happy lives in Washington DC or Virginia. Our town was
no exception. We were proud to say that our Cumberland
County had the great, great, great, great, great grandson
of Abraham Lincoln living and working in our town. And
he looked just like him.

His name was ABRAHAM LINCOLN THE 12TH and he
worked over at the Pep Boys Auto Care as a service tech-
nician. The Pep Boys (for those that don't know) is a fine
automotive shop that fixes cars, repairs trucks, sells bat-
teries and floor mats. They have an excellent nationwide
reputation and I have taken my car there many times
and been pleased. Once I bought the ex wife an anniver-
sary gift of a pine cone air freshener which lasted longer
then our marriage. (She is now married to a woman
named Olestra and working as a corrections guard at a
maximum security prison in Tennessee. I see her on
occasion. We still have memories.)

Back to my story: Abraham Lincoln the 12th worked
over at the Pep Boys like I said. He would look over your
car when you brought it in and tell you what was wrong
with it. Oh sure he looked like Abraham Lincoln our 16th
President. He had the beard and the mole and was tall
and lanky and wore the stove pipe hat with his Pep Boys
uniform. He had "Abraham Lincoln" sewn on his shirt on
his Pep Boys uniform. Some of the beard dropped off on
your car and the mole was cancerous looking but damn if
he didn't look just like the 16th President of the United
States. That was his claim to fame and he was treated

with utter respect and dignity in Cumberland County by all the townspeople. They would call him Abraham Lincoln the 12th, or Abraham Lincoln Jr., or Abe, or Mr. President, or the Great Emancipator. He sure could fix cars and his prices were fair and he was honest. That's what folks referred to him in Cumberland County as: Honest Abe The Pep Boys Service Manager. One fella called him Scott. But that was because he was jealous. "He may be the direct descendant of Abraham Lincoln but he is NOT Abraham Lincoln," said this fella. (I think his name was Ric Nibble). "So, I'll just call him Scott."

Abraham Lincoln the 12th was a real fixture around town walking around in his long black coat with his stovepipe hat when he was not working at the Pep Boys. He would shop at the local K-Mart and buy normal things—socks and shower curtains and mothballs and it was like watching Abraham Lincoln shopping. He would move his shopping cart up the aisle at K-Mart and all the shoppers would nod to him or give him a "Hello, Mr. President," and "Nice Gettysburg speech," and so on. I guess folks were just tongue tied to meet a celebrity and just said anything.

Well, wouldn't you know it. The great, great, great, great grandson of George Washington moved into our town one summer. Yes, that's what I'm saying. GEORGE WASHINGTON THE 24TH came to Cumberland County to live and that sure was something.

He looked just like George Washington our ex-president. He had the white powdered wig, and the stretchy purple colonial pants, and the ruffly shirt, and the Mona Lisa smile. You swore you were looking at George Washington. And why not? This was the direct descendant, authentic blood, the actual drippings, the bonafide stickies of George Washington our first President right here in Cumberland County working at the local Home Depot home improvement store selling you fans and patio furniture and answering your questions about wood stains and patio umbrellas.

Let me just say here that Home Depot is one of the finest home improvement stores in our great nation. It's a chain and they are very good. Good prices, service, and selection. I have never failed to be pleased while shopping there. So . . . when I looked in the window and I saw what I thought to be George Washington bending over with an extension cord near a fat man's foot I was shocked. (No pun intended) I said to myself, "Is that George Washington? Ready to plug in a lamp near a fat man's foot? That sure is a fat man's foot and that sure looks like George Washington. Is it him?"

And the Home Depot manager must have heard me because he said to me "It's his descendant. It's his great grandson 24th removed. He works here."

I said "He's working here?"

And he said "Yes. He's one of our best service attendants. Very knowledgeable. Works the afternoon shift. Need an extension cord today?"

Oh, he sure knew his stuff alright. George Washington the 24th could talk up a storm about Homer Ornsbys Deck Stain, and latex blends, and varnish, and canvas coverings, and tiny screws, and big nuts. Stains, screws, latex, and nuts. Those were his specialities. At work he wore a Home Depot uniform which was the Khaki pants, Hush Puppy shoes, and Home Depot vest with his name tag on it that said "George Washington". But you called him George, or Georgie, or GW, or Washy, or Mr. Washington. One guy called him Scott which was, I guess, his retaliation of some sort. His jealousy, I guess.

"It's not him. It may be a relative but he's not George Washington THE President of the United States. So why should I call him George Washington?" was this fella's answer. (I think his name was Ric Nibble). "So I'll just call him Scott."

Well, the day had to come. Abraham Lincoln the 12th was trying on shoes at the local Thom McCann. Surprisingly although he was 6'5" he had a tiny foot (size fives) and he must have had about fifteen pairs of shoes out walking back and forth and wiggling into shoes, crunching his toes and crossing his legs and his mole was getting bigger and the shoe salesman said it was discoloring even while he was there trying on shoes.

And who walks in? None other then George Washington the 24th. He was wearing shorts and a t-shirt but he still had his powdered wig on. The two of them just stared at each other. It was a sight to see. They eyed each other like a matador and a bull, like 2 dogs on a lawn. I mean after all this was the direct descendants of George Washington and Abraham Lincoln right here in Cumberland County. Working and living. Eye to eye.

Well . . . they just stared at each other. They did nothing, they said nothing. George Washington the 24th simply tried on a pair of moccasins, liked them, then went to the register to pay for them. He pulled out 38 one dollar bills and paid the clerk as Lincoln the 12th eyed him.

I'm sure he saw George Washington's portrait on those dollar bills. Lincoln locked eyes with Washington as he passed each one of those dollar bills from his hand to the clerk's hand. Their eyes never left each other. George Washington the 24th just smiled that Mona Lisa smile of his.

Then Lincoln the 12th scooped up the shoes he wanted and went to the register. (I think they were loafers). He paid the clerk with 6 five dollar bills as Washington watched. Oh sure, I'm positive Washington saw Abraham Lincoln's portrait on each five dollar bill as it passed from the hand of Lincoln to the clerk. Lincoln smiled a trumped you kind of smile but their eyes never left each other.

And then for good measure Abraham Lincoln the 12th put a penny in each loafer. Well . . . Washington the 24th pulled out a quarter and said, "Even."

Then he left. He walked out of the Thom McCann shoe store as the bell let out a little tinkle.

That is my story I hope you like it. Next time I will tell you about JAN WILKES BOOTH—the great, great, great, great, great granddaughter of John Wilkes Booth working in Cumberland County at the local Ford dealership. (Near the theater).

DanceTeacher

Ed Broth
10153 1/2 Riverside Dr. #24
Toluca Lake, CA 91602

September 3, 2003

Dear Mr. Broth,

Thank you so much for submitting your story, FAMOUS DESCENDANTS to *Dance Teacher*, and we are thrilled that you are a fan of the magazine! Unfortunately, the submission does not meet our needs at this time.

Best wishes,

Associate Editor
Dance Teacher magazine

PART 3 OF THE HOTEL
HONOR BAR STORY

I am now nearing the end of the book you are reading as I travel this great country of ours. To refresh: I am a traveling salesman. A pretty darn good one. I think. I work for the DENNIE RESTAURANT chain. I go through company records matching up racial incidents with company apologies to see which ones we can and can't use again. It's my duty to go through records and find the restaurant which had the racial outburst and then see what corporate statement we issued to temper it. To date there have been 1312 racial outbursts and 1312 statements of apologies. We don't want to mistakenly apologize if we have used that apology before. So you can see I am pretty busy on the road with this.

I drive a Chevy Mostaccioli. This is Chevy's sportiest car and I have told them so. In my letter to them I said: "I am quite happy with my Chevy Mostaccioli. It is sporty. I bought it used. I traded in a Honda Veal N' Pasta which, while giving me great gas mileage, smelled". It was some sort of an Italian food odor that lingered. I do not know what. But Honda is a great car!

Tonight I find myself in Mommy, Ohio. I'm staying at THE RADISH-SON NGUYEN PHAP NIEM HOTEL. Nobody puts out a finer hotel then the Radish-son. This is a chain hotelery that meets all expectations of travelers. (Of which I am one) Let me just say here that the Nguyen Phap Niem Hotel is a superb place. I have enjoyed many nights in this chain hotel around the country where I have entertained business associates, conventioneers, corporate functions, and the occasional chubby lady from Sacramento who I see whenever I get a chance. Although

I am not a Chubby Chaser. Her name is Cheryl. Cheryl Glimpsey, you will remember, and she likes to shove a lot of crackers into her mouth at once then open her mouth at me. I say "Take a drink of water." Once I saw her take a shower in a sink at a Phoenix rest stop. She put her big toe in the faucet and maneuvered the spray onto herself that way.

TO CONTINUE: At the check-in desk they called my name: "Mr. Broth, your room is ready" as they handed me a key. To my left was another traveler just checking in. "My name is Joe Consume'," said the traveler. "I believe I have a reservation."

We eyed each other. But said nothing. The encounter passed without incident.

I must say this is a courteous and caring hotel. The manager is an old friend named Nat King. And he has cole slaw that is delicious. I told him "You should package this stuff and sell it, that's how good it is." I always ask for the Nat King Cole Slaw whenever I'm at the Radish-son Nguyen Phap Niem Hotel. Every time I see Nat he says "Hit me in the stomach. Go ahead pound me in the bread basket. I do a thousand leg crunches a day. Whack me in the pouch. I do 1200 ab scrinches an hour." Once I did hit him and he winced and doubled over. I said "You told me to hit you."

And he said "You didn't give me a chance to tighten my stomach." Then he threw a bag of sod at me in the lobby.

BACK TO MY HONOR BAR STORY: In my hotel room, I noticed that my mini bar was stocked with expensive snacks and soft drinks. I was intrigued. The thought of paying $67.00 for a soda and some nuts interested me. I was pondering this when I heard a scuffle in the room next to mine. I went out into the hall. The door to the next room was open and the Radish-son Nguyen Phap

Niem Security was wrestling one of the guests to the
floor. Apparently he tried to beat their Honor Bar System. The hotel had installed a laser beam across the mini
bar to prevent theft. If you cross into the honor bar area
and do not pay, it will shock you like a taser gun. This
guest tried to take the back off the TV and go into the
Honor Bar that way. From what I understand, he
crawled under the laser beam, took 4 small screws off
the back of the TV, used a wire hanger, and tried to
remove a Famous Amos for free. But the stun taser
zapped him and disabled the TV, the Honor Bar, and also
caused a red welt on his arm. This was a signal for the
Radish-son Nguyen Phap Niem Security to move in. They
appeared at his hotel room door like a Prison Interven-
tion Team then burst in. They got him onto to the floor,
each man taking a leg or an arm, then into the hallway,
and hustled him down the steps and into a waiting police
cruiser. I watched the whole thing. I snacked on a
Toblerone Bar. (For which I did not pay.) The Security
Guard acknowledged me as he took the perpetrator out. I
gave him a semi blink, he gave me a knowing concur-
rence.

I later found out that the suite on the other side of
mine was outfitted with a monitoring system: cameras
and microphones and a room full of cops to see and hear
the mini bar offender. "Mini bar thieves are the vile of
the universe, the scum of the world," the Nguyen Phap
Niem Hotel manager said to me. "Do not tempt us."

I concur. Hotel people are fierce. They will hunt you
down like a dog. They will follow you to the ends of the
earth if you screw with them. They are vicious people,
these hotel people. (But they are not stupes)

I stepped into the evening. Perhaps to the lounge.

September 8, 2003

Ed Broth
10153 ½ Riverside Dr. # 241
Toluca Lake, CA 91602

Dear Mr. Broth:

We are in receipt of your recent letter and thank you for taking the time to write. Everyone's day seems to be so very busy and it is truly a pleasure to hear from someone who takes the time to express his or her opinion.

Honda is concerned with customer satisfaction, and we strive daily to improve the quality of service we provide to our customers before and after the sale. Your impressions are appreciated and considered.

Parmesan Stain ↓

We have documented your comments regarding the odor in your previous vehicle and have made the proper departments aware of your comments for future reference. Unfortunately, we do not have any suggestions for you on how to get rid of a lingering food odor. If you have any additional questions or comments, please feel free to call us at (800) 382-2238 during normal business hours.

We look forward to a long and successful association with you.

Sincerely,

SERVICE OPERATIONS

Automobile Customer Service

Honda Automobile Division

American Honda Motor Company, Inc., 1919 Torrance Boulevard, Torrance, California 90501-2746 Phone (310) 783-2000

B16 SATURDAY, AUGUST 16, 2003 SF   The Tampa Herald

OBITUARIES/FUNERAL ANNOUNCEMENTS

RUDY DELAPEEP, 77; FORMER CARNIVAL, CONTORTIONIST. CURRENT GOVERNOR OF BIBB COUNTY.

*"Could Bend Himself
In Many Shapes"*

Honolulu Hank

Governor Delapeep

Rudy Broth, better known as Rudy Delapeep, a colorful contortionist who made a living for many years on the carnival circuit has died. Delapeep succumbed in his hospital bed of the Al Pacino Stool. Governor Delapeep could bend himself in many shapes always to the amusement and amazement of the audiences. He was a staple in carnivals and circuses for many years before winning election as Governor of Bibb County. "He delighted so many," said former carnival performer Honolulu Hank. "I had the chance to do a show with him in Colorado. He had over 27 bends." As Governor, Delapeep passed the No Shoes, No Shirt, No Service Law in restaurants. Which the singing group S*it, Shower, and Shave adapted, recorded, and made into a big #2. (Hit record) "Because everyone was eating without any shirts or shoes on in all the restaurants," said Chief Of Staff Marco Radish. Commenting on his death, Menohar Goopi of the prestigious Goopta-Goopi Clinic in Seafood, New Mexico said, "Once we saw the Al Pacino face in his stool he was a goner. It is a deadly stool from which there is no recovery." Delapeep leaves his glittery contortionist's costume to nephew Ed Broth. Services are pending. The body can be viewed at the local Olive Garden Restaurant while the Bibb County Mortuary is being remodeled.

DEADLY STOOL

The Tampa Herald

TO: COLUMBIA UNIVERSITY

FROM: Ed Broth

Please accept my work
"THE GENE RAYBURN STORY" for
consideration for your Pulitzer Prize for
Literature Award

THE GENE RAYBURN STORY

I was watching "Match Game" on TV the other day (Channel 1,204). Let me say here now that I have the full cable package. I used to just get the free Network Channels 2, 4, and 7 and maybe Channel 5 and Channel 13. Now I have 347 Korean Channels and 702 Spanish channels. Since I don't speak Spanish or Korean I flip through them. But I pay for them each month. No fool am I.

Back to my story: I was watching "The Match Game" on TV like I said. The host of "The Match Game" was Gene Rayburn and I realized that nobody cares about Gene Rayburn anymore. I mean you could go out onto the streets and ask 100 people who Gene Rayburn is and nobody would know. So what does it all mean? What did Gene Rayburn mean to anybody? What good is it all? And Gene Rayburn at least got to be the host of the "Match Game." That was an accomplishment to some people at least. There are plenty of people who would at least say "Yes, hosting the Match Game and being Gene Rayburn is an accomplishment. Sure. I have never hosted the Match Game nor have I been on TV so, yes, that would be an accomplishment." (Try it. Go out onto the street and strike up a Gene Rayburn conversation with a stranger; see if they say it.)

25 years ago Gene Rayburn could walk into The Red Lobster Restaurant and people would rush around. "Yes, Mr. Rayburn, right away, Mr. Rayburn, I saw you on "Match Game" today. Can I get you a complimentary crab appetizer, Mr. Rayburn? May I empty your ashtray, Mr. Rayburn. May I bow to your celebrity and give away our crabs and seat you ahead of the others, Mr. Rayburn?" That was the life of celebrity Gene Rayburn 25 years ago. Today it is: "Gene Rayburn's coming in." The 22 year old foreign manager would say "Who is she? I don't know a Gene Rayburn. Is she with the woman's group that called?" And then you explain to her that Gene Rayburn was the host of the "Match Game" and that she would say, "What is that, is that an old TV show? We can't give away free crab appetizers. We can't empty anyone's ash tray." So what does it all mean, what good is it? At one time I wished I was him. I died to be Gene Rayburn. Today? I don't give a darn to be Gene Rayburn. So now when I watch "Match Game" on TV Land from 1973 I realize what a flop Gene Rayburn turned out to be and how little he really meant to any of us. He with his long microphone, and crab stained dentures, and witty banter with Charles Nelson Reilly who is also a nothing. The two of them can bow to me. And I'm not a celebrity. Gene Rayburn is a nothing in my eyes.

PART 2 OF THE GENE RAYBURN STORY

The man came into the restaurant every day for a week. I immediately recognized him as Gene Rayburn from the old 1973 "Match Game" TV show. It was now 29 years later and he still looked the same. "I'll have a Baboon Melt to go," he said to me in that unmistakable Gene Rayburn voice. I said "You're Gene Rayburn aren't you?" He looked at me with watery eyes and said in his most bellowing voice: "Yes. Yes I am. I am Gene Rayburn!! he bellowed. "I used to be somebody! I am so pleased that you recognized me. I have not been on TV since 1973 and it is truly a a privilege to be recognized by you, a foreign restaurant manager." He then commented that he always liked the Red Lobster Restaurant. He liked the food, ambience, people, and prices. "Make sure that Baboon Melt is dry," he said. I gave him a nod he followed with a tug. Gene Rayburn had brought a manatee in with him to the restaurant. He told me he had caught this manatee off the Florida coast and that it was his friend and smelled but he still liked schlepping it around. I told him that we don't allow fish in the restaurant and he got up to me real close with his watery Basset Hound eyes and his hot potato salad breath and he said "This is a fish restaurant isn't it? NOW SEAT ME AND MY MANATEE!" And I have to admit he had a point. Even though at that moment I knew that Gene Rayburn had slipped into level 5 dementia*.

I looked at this Gene Rayburn and wondered about him on the "Match Game". What had become of him,

---

*Level 5 Dementia: slipping into a Gene Rayburn like state.

dragging a smelly manatee around and looking for food? He was a bum in my eyes. A zero. A zilch. I realized for a 2nd time that Gene Rayburn was a nothing. He never was and he never will be. After all was said and done, the "Match Game" meant nothing. Gene Rayburn was truly just a poppyseed in this life. A speck. A blot. A smudge, a soil. (If indeed it even was Gene Rayburn. Because later on the busboy said he had his doubts that this was THE Gene Rayburn. He said it was a Gene Rayburn impostor that's been seen in the parking lot before. I believed him. Gene Rayburn is at least a classy man. This was NOT Gene Rayburn. I could never believe it. But who would go to the trouble of impersonating Gene Rayburn?)

COLUMBIA UNIVERSITY IN THE CITY OF NEW YORK
THE PULITZER PRIZES

Thank you for the interest you have shown in The Pulitzer Prizes.

Unfortunately, the material you submitted is not eligible for prize consideration for the following reason(s):

only published books are eligible

The Pulitzer Prize Plan of Award is enclosed for your information.

```
To: BUTTMAN MAGAZINE

From: Ed Broth

Please accept my work "THE GENE RAYBURN STORY"
for consideration in your BUTTMAN magazine.
```

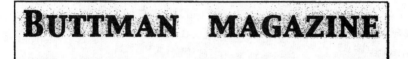

BUTTMAN MAGAZINE

– To Buttman Magazine Contributor –

Thank you for your recent submission! However, we are unable to use it at this time, and are returning it to you.

We encourage you to send in other pieces of original art.

Thank you for your continued interest!

The Editors

We cannot use your story because there was no sexual content, and it (the story) had no relevance to Buttman Magazine.

TO: BUTTMAN MAGAZINE

FROM: Ed Broth

Please accept "PART 3 OF THE GENE RAYBURN STORY".
I must admit that I also submitted this story to the
PULIZTER PRIZE AWARD FOR LITERATURE. If the Pulitzer
prize accepts, I cannot place this into Buttman, as they
are very prestigious. However, I do have another story to
submit to you. That story is called "CONJUGAL CAL".

PART 3 OF THE GENE RAYBURN STORY

Marley was dead: to begin with. There is no doubt whatever about that. The register of his burial was signed by
his clergyman, the clerk, the undertaker, and the chief
mourner. Scrooge signed it: and Scrooge's name was good
upon 'Change, for anything he chose to put his hand to.
Marley was dead as a door-nail.

I had always wanted to start a story the way Charles
Dickens did in "A Christmas Carol" and I thought "Part 3
Of The Gene Rayburn Story" deserved it. After all, this
was a Pulitzer Prize piece of work. (My story—not Dickens)

So with that in mind I started my story off:

Gene Rayburn liked big butts: to begin with. There
was no doubt whatever about that. Gene Rayburn was a

butt man. He told me so. He said "I like big butts on women." It was as simple as that. He liked 'em big and he liked 'em on women. The register at the hotel said it: Gene Rayburn and big butted woman-1 night. The register was signed by the clergyman, the clerk, the undertaker, and the chief mourner. Scrooge signed it. And Scrooge was the manager of the Comfort Inn. And Scrooge's name was good upon 'Change, for anything he chose to put his hand to. Gene Rayburn liked big butts.

"I like big butted women. I don't care what the rest of them looks like! I don't even care where their butts are on them! If they're on their back that's great. Because I am a butt man!!!! That's why I read Buttman Magazine." Gene would tell me this over and over again as I picked him up for his ride to "LEE'S WIDE FEET" to buy shoes. Gene had abnormally wide feet. He wore a triple E, size 6 shoe. Small wide feet, that's what he had. Maybe that's why he liked big butts. But then again, who doesn't? Huh? (Like big butts)

Gene came into the Red Lobster Restaurant often. Although the Bus Boy said to me, "Man, that's not Gene Rayburn. Gene Rayburn has pink hair." Who knew if it was Gene Rayburn or not? It could have been just been a pink haired man that looked like Gene Rayburn but one thing I knew, was what I heard from who I thought was Gene Rayburn: "I like 'em big. Butts that is. And so does my Manatee. We're butt persons." He schlepped that manatee with him wherever he went. Once I saw him on the street hitching with that damn fish. Just standing on the side of the road with that stupid looking sea otter on a leash. They were just standing there, Gene with his thumb out and his pink hair on top of his head. He said the manatee's name was Clancy but I knew it as Clark. I had seen that manatee in the restaurant before. It came in a lot. Why not? It was a seafood restaurant.

Clark ⟶

To continue with Part 3 Of The Gene Rayburn Story—
The Butt Fetish:

Believe it or not somebody picked them up as they hitched! I watched out of the corner of my eye as a car slowed down in front of them then stopped. Gene ran over to the car tugging Clark with him. They got into the car and wouldn't you know it? Guess what? It was a big butted woman that gave them a ride. "I like 'em big!!!" Gene bellowed onto the Freeway as they drove away. "Give me a large or small woman but make sure her butt is big!!! he was heard to say as the car roared down the street. (He may have been binge drinking, but I don't know. All I know is he yelled at the top of his lungs. "IS THERE ANY MORE PRETZELS?") Then he passed out on the side of the road. Went down in 4 steps like Ikea shelving.

One day Henry Kiplinger came into the restaurant. He ordered haliBUTT. But that's another story for Buttman Magazine. Later on I'll finish this story.

ED BROTH
10153 ½ Riverside Dr. #241
Toluca Lake, CA 91602

Editor Nick Evangelista
Fencers Quarterly Magazine
848 S. Kimbrough
Springfield, MO 65806
Sep 10, 2003

Dear Editor Evangelista,

I have had many a month to really think about what you said regarding my stories. I want to start off by sincerely thanking you for taking the time to write me back about my writing. I want you to know that I appreciate your advice. I showed others here in the wash area after the afternoon wash up your many letters of encouragement and they felt I should send you a new story because I can make progress. I can place a story. I focused this time. I really focused. Thank you for being a really caring editor and helping those that need it. Others here say you are really a good person to care about those who try. I showed one man an Italian tile. Fencing is wonderful. The swordplay is wonderful. I have seen The 3 Musketeers on TV. It teaches us quite a bit about sports and fairmenship and moving around.

Now down to my new story. I have removed any references to convicts and underwear as you suggested. This new story, I feel, really captures the fencing angle you are seeking. Some stories are about fencing action and some are just about the life of a fencer. I hope you can see what I mean when you read it.

I want to order a subscription because I think this fencing sport will help us all. How do I do that?

Mr. Evangelista, thank you again sir, for your consideration. And for helping those that need it. I hope you like my new story. I look forward to your advice. I am trying.

Respectfully,

Ed Broth

Ed T. Broth

THE FENCER WHO RETURNED
SHORTY PAJAMAS
TO THE STORE

The man came into the store every morning at 10 when they opened. He always had a shopping bag with him and in that bag was a pair of shorty pajamas. When he approached the register, the clerk said "Can I help you?"

And the man would take the shorty pajamas out of the bag and say to the clerk, "I would like to return these shorty pajamas."

And the clerk would say "Is there a problem with your shorty pajamas?"

And the man would say "No. I just want to return them."

And the clerk would cheerfully take the shorty pajamas from the man and make out the return paperwork as the man said "While you do that I'll be over here shopping." Then the man would shop as the clerk was doing the return. Then the man would come back to the clerk's register with a new pair of shorty pajamas and say "I would like to buy this new pair of shorty pajamas."

And the clerk would say, "Very well, sir. They are a good choice of shorty pajamas you have there. Our finest. I'll ring them up for you." Then the clerk would ring up the man's shorty pajamas on the register and put them in a new shopping bag and give them to the man who would be on his way. I think this man was a fencer or fencing instructor. He seemed to be. The way he stood there in a regal fencing pose with his shorty pajamas ready to purchase. Fencing is a fine sport and I recommend it to everyone. If you haven't tried it you really should.

The next morning the man would come into the store and go to the register and pull out the shorty pajamas that he bought yesterday from his shopping bag and say "I want to return these shorty pajamas."

And the clerk would say "Is there something wrong with your shorty pajamas?"

And the man would say, "No, I just want to return them."

And the clerk would say, "Very well, sir, glad to do it. I can help you here." And then he would take the shorty pajamas from the man and do the return as the man said, "I'll just be shopping over here by your register as you do that." While the clerk was processing the return, the man would come back to the register with a new pair of shorty pajamas and say "I'd like to buy these."

And the clerk would say, "Those are very nice shorty pajamas, good choice, sir, I'm sure you'll like them. They're our finest. Very nice cotton-polyester blend." Then he would ring up the sale and the man would be on his way with his new pair of shorty pajamas.

The next day the man came back to the store and returned the shorty pajamas. He did this for 12 days in a row. Always buying a pair of shorty pajamas and always returning them the next day. This man told the clerk that he enjoyed fencing and the competitiveness of the fencing sport, the wiggling around with the twangy sword, the masks, and the stretchy fencing pants the fencers wore. He said "I like this stuff." And the clerk nodded a nod of agreement and acceptance. (You could tell this clerk also liked fencing.)

One day the clerk said to the man, "Why do you always buy a new pair of shorty pajamas and then return them the next day?"

And the man said, "Because they get stinky. I sleep in them at night and they get stinky the next morning and

I wash them out in my sink. I buy them because I need shorty pajamas to sleep in. But I can't put them on my clothesline to dry so I just return them and buy a new pair of shorty pajamas.

And the clerk said, "Why can't you put them on your clothesline to dry?"

And the man said, "Because my neighbor is a bastard who thinks my shorty pajamas are waving to him when they are simply flapping in the wind drying." (His name is Frank Tint.) He said they were the Devil. I said "Nonsense. How can a pair of shorty pajamas be the Devil? They are simply shorty pajamas flapping in the wind drying. Not waving." What is he insane? My neighbor also said he enjoyed fencing and dancing around with swords that bend and twang. And putting on the meshy mask. "I like this stuff," he said. Hey, who doesn't?

I went on to tell this clerk that it's stupid for me to wash them out at night because I can't hang them out to dry on my clothesline because of my neighbor. (That bastard Frank Tint). So I have to buy a new pair every day, sleep in them and get them stinky, then return them and buy a new pair. It's as simple as that. There was people fencing around this clerk. (As you can see by the photos enclosed). They were parrying and swishing with their swords. It's a great sport! Everything about it is exciting! They asked for the fencing apparel section of the store and the clerk graciously directed them and said "I just took up fencing myself. I can recommend a good magazine if you like. It's loaded with informative articles and has wonderful pictures of men squatting in stretchy pants and has nice ads and the editor's column is very good." (The clerk said all that)

I went on to tell this clerk that I had my shorty pajamas on my clothesline and my ingrate of a neighbor gave me such grief because they were flapping and waving to him and destroying his family that I won't even have them in my yard. (Not even near my clothesline let alone on it) I told this clerk my shorty pajamas were flapping to get dry (not waving) and one day they even winked at me. I said my neighbor was mistaken.

And the clerk said to me "Are they the Devil?"

And I said "Nonsense. How can a pair of shorty pajamas be the Devil? They are simply shorty pajamas getting clean after a night of sleeping in them. (They get stinky) The Devil is someone that tortures someone and is evil. How can a story about shorty pajamas torture someone and be evil to someone? Huh?"

The fencer did not shop in the store after that. He went back to the great sport of fencing. A sport which teaches us a lesson each time we fence. What's better than that? Everyone should try fencing. I know I will. I hope you enjoy the photos I took of that day in the store.

END

Fencing Gear For the Brain

FENCERS QUARTERLY

MAGAZINE

848 S. Kimbrough,
Springfield, MO 65806

Dear Ed:

    Still, no! You could tack one hundred fencing pictures onto this short story, and it still wouldn't be about fencing. If you know nothing about fencing or swords, you shouldn't even try selling to us. Reading that sample of *FQM* I sent you should have told you this.

    Buy yourself a copy of *Writer's Market* (every serious writer should have one), and try other magazines. Preferably general interest magazines.

    Please do not send this story to us again.

Sincerely,

Nick Evangelista

Nick Evangelista

Editor-in-Chief